# Gotta Do Somethin' 'Bout That Dog!

by

## Frederick Woodard
## Canine Behaviorist and Master Trainer
## with Kathleen Kellaway

authorHOUSE

1663 LIBERTY DRIVE, SUITE 200
BLOOMINGTON, INDIANA 47403
(800) 839-8640
www.authorhouse.com

First published by AuthorHouse 09/18/04

ISBN: 1-4184-0010-6 (e)
ISBN: 1-4184-0011-4 (sc)

This book is printed on acid-free paper.

Printed in the United States of America
Bloomington, Indiana

# ACKNOWLEDGMENTS

My grateful thanks to:

*Robert Dolan*: Mentor from my early days and friend to the end. Thanks, Bob, for teaching me from the very beginning.

*"CJ"*: My longsuffering office manager. You've helped keep the business in business all these years. Thanks for your dedication, loyalty, hard work, and even longer hours!

*The K-9 Concepts Staff:* Thanks for hitting the road and helping to make the business successful. Your hard work is much appreciated.

*The K-9 Concepts Students and Alumni:* Thank you for the opportunity to work with you and your dogs, and for your dedicated effort to "do somethin' 'bout that dog!"

*My Canine Students:* This book would not have been possible without all of you, from miniature pinschers to Dobermans. Thanks for showing us humans your potential and how very bright and versatile you all are. Hopefully, this book will help us to understand and appreciate you.

# TABLE OF CONTENTS

# WARNING!

I believe that you really love your dog and want to learn about him. If that's the case, there can be no room for denial. This book was written for those who have a real desire to learn about canine behavior, and it is not for the squeamish, nor for those who only want to read fuzzy puppy stories. The information in this book covers the gamut from happy endings to some horror stories, but education is everything. Ultimately, knowledge keeps us safe.

Working with dogs for more than 22 years, I can tell you that truth should be your goal. There can be some ugly truths in dealing with dogs, but learning about canine behavior averts catastrophes that others have experienced simply by insisting upon doing things their own way. Some of the things I will share with you may shock you, but bear in mind that closing our eyes and covering our ears never got us anywhere but in for a rude awakening.

In today's world, we can still enjoy dogs as we desire. However, we need to also recognize that our liabilities have changed dramatically over the past decade. Generally, we are quite responsible for our dog's interactions, good or bad. If you are having problems with your dog, and you've tried just about everything you thought possible, these instructions are designed to get the results you desire. You've *"Gotta Do Somethin' 'Bout That Dog!"*

# INTRODUCTION

"Canis lupus": Wolf. A flesh-eating mammal. "Canis lupus familiaris":

Your dog. Descended from wolves. The dog you have chosen to bring home with you or the dog residing with you and your family now is all that. Whether fluffy puppy or hulking Shepherd, these "pets" are anything but tame on the inside. The key to living comfortably with your dog is understanding what he is made of and what makes him tick. It is a disservice to yourself and your dog to treat him as though he is like you in the mental, physical, or emotional realms. After all, the main goal in adopting a dog is to keep him with you for his lifetime, and this can sometimes last as long as 15 years. Doesn't it make sense to understand exactly what is living in your home, in close personal contact with you for such a length of time? Knowledge of your dog is everything to you as his owner, and he cannot sit down and discuss the reasons why he is who he is. That responsibility is up to you. If you love your dog, you will teach him. To teach him, you must know all about him.

Discovering what your dog is all about is the purpose of this book. It will explore not only the mental and physiological makeup of canines, but also a unique process by which they can be conditioned and trained to become obedient members of your household. Many are misled by desiring to own a dog merely for companionship. Your dog is capable of much more than you ever dreamed. The training process which will be explained will bring about not only obedience and control, but also develop guarding and protection abilities, both valuable assets to you and your family. Your dog is not just a dog. Let's delve into his mind and makeup to learn about some of those "animal instincts."

# CHAPTER I:
# THE CANINE MIND

We will begin with a very basic question: ***What is a pack?***

A pack is a formed group of dogs that co-exists and works together. They group together in the wild for safety and breeding purposes. They hunt together, protect each other, and provide companionship for each other. In order for them to live together peacefully, they must have an understood set of rules. The most important of these rules is the establishment of the "pecking order," or "hierarchy."

In canine hierarchy, the most dominant dog would be the female, or "alpha dog." The others will follow her in order of dominance, with the "alpha male" ranking second in command. Any newcomers to the established pack must follow the laws and pecking order of the pack.

Some of these pack laws involve hunting, mating, and food consumption practices. For example, none of the pack members, even puppies, are able to simply eat at leisure. Alpha female is always first. After a kill, she consumes her portion and regurgitates the partially digested food for her pups. If a pup makes an attempt to assert his right to eat whenever he feels like it, he will be met with solid eye contact and a meaningful growl by Mama, followed by a "scruff" correction. If necessary, this process will be repeated more violently. Submissive urination follows correction together with a change of attitude!

Mating is the strictest of all pack laws, survival of the species being the instinctive drive behind it. Mating between the healthiest, most dominant alpha dogs ensures healthy physical and mental propagation of the species. This type of instinctive breeding actually keeps disease down and circumvents the harmful results of inbreeding, such as physical and mental insufficiency. The female alpha chooses the strongest male for herself.

It is quite common for established members to occasionally challenge for pecking order status. The challenged member must make his opposition submit in order to retain his status within the pack. Threat postures are undertaken at this point, consisting of the tail held in an upright position, a snarl which exposes only the canines and a few front teeth, and the scruff on the neck and back raised. If the challenger is bested and submits, all is well in his world. If he refuses, he is expelled from the pack – a lonely renegade who hunts and survives alone until and unless he is able to establish membership within another roving pack.

In the wild, canines dig holes in the ground and claim them as "den areas." Very basically, these dens allow them to keep warm, keep cool, breed, and survive. They will defend their dens violently if necessary. Later, I will discuss den areas in detail in relation to *your* den – where you live.

# CHAPTER 2:
# SHOULD I BOTHER TO TRAIN MY DOG?

Training is more than just teaching your dog to obey. Contrary to the thinking of many, training is not negative interaction. After all, we cannot allow our children *or* our dogs to do exactly as they please. This type of scenario would, and does, create chaos. Just as there is order in our world, there should be order in theirs, particularly because we, as parents of children and owners of dogs, are ultimately responsible for whatever consequences may arise. Teaching your dog is a fun process with the proper attitude. He will amaze you with his level of intelligence. You both will benefit as a result of teaching. You will never be sorry you invested the time and patience to train. It is called "discipline," and we need it just as much as our dogs do. Conditioning your dog with the correct interaction increases his intelligence, confidence, spirit, and judge of character. It enhances all of your dog's innate good qualities. Training is not just "heel" and "sit" on a leash; rather, it is a way of life, the way in which you properly interact with your dog for the duration of his life.

From the tiniest miniature Schnauzer to a Doberman, no one wants an animal diving on her when arriving at her friend's door. Pantyhose aren't cheap. Grandma tends to take exception to being imprinted in the wall behind the front door. And who really enjoys having to push a dog down or away constantly during a visit? How about being "nipped"? Many professionals have no knowledge of the "nip". We do know that there are only higher and higher levels if this practice is allowed to continue. When you want something done, you simply want it done. It is much easier to achieve high levels of obedience by training your dog than it is by teaching our own children. Much quicker, too, I might add, for a dog who is being conditioned learns by repetition. For example, when you tell your dog to sit, he will sit every time when properly trained. And since life is hard enough, why have a major war with your family dog on a daily basis? It isn't necessary.

Another issue with an untrained dog is unpredictability. Can you put your dog on a "wait" and know he'll stay there until told that he can move? Can you trust him to leave the steak on the table alone if you turn your back? Do you trust him alone with your two-year-old? Would you like to stop chasing your dog down the block every time the door is opened? Wouldn't you love to be able to? A properly-trained dog is a joy to live with. There are no surprises, only predictable behavior – the rules of your home which you have instilled in him.

Training also builds a bond with your dog and fosters his protective instinct toward you and your family. Did you ever have someone in your past, perhaps Dad, Grandpa, or Uncle Bob, who taught you things you would never have known without his direction? He was patient with you and went over the procedure many times if you needed it. He praised you when you did well and corrected you if you fell short. Ultimately, you learned. A bond was forged between the two of you – teacher and student. You respected him and wanted to please. That's your gold mine right there. Training your dog will teach him to respect you. He already has a natural desire to please. That's a win-win combination. You need only invest your time and patience to achieve the desired results.

Friends enjoy visiting. Grandma's not afraid to come over. No one has to fight the dog at the dinner table. If you take your training far enough, imagine your pride on the field or in the street, when only non-verbal commands, or hand signals, cause your dog to sit, down, or freeze in motion. This level of control is not only to be highly respected, but can be a lifesaver to both your dog and/or someone else in certain situations.

# CHAPTER 3:
# THINGS YOU DON'T WANT TO DO TO YOUR DOG

Let's explore some negatives and positives regarding the way most people live with their dogs. Like all of us, you have probably been asked many times, "I have good news and bad news. Which do you want first?" Although answers may vary, I am going to begin with the negatives, or what *not* to do. However, every story should have a happy ending, and this one is no exception.

## *WRONG THING #1: MY DOG IS MY BABY*

Remember the definition of *Canis lupus familiaris?* Yes, dogs, especially puppies, are soft, cuddly, and cute. That's pretty much where the similarity ends. Let us study the term "*anthropomorphism* ". This is the infliction of human reasoning upon animals that cannot understand our emotional roller coasters and inconsistent interaction. Cruelty results when we hold them accountable. How can a dog comprehend why he can jump on Dad and teenage son, but not Mom? Is the behavior acceptable or isn't it? We must learn to separate our human reasoning and emotions from our dealings with canines. They are like oil and water. When we try to instill humanistic values into our interaction with dogs, damaging consequences could and usually do follow. Examples of this will be given later, with stories of experiences you can relate to. It's far too easy to see.

Overcoddling. Although much easier to do with smaller breeds, many people unknowingly put this into practice, even with puppies who will later become huge adult canines. Overcoddling wears many faces, one being excessive attention and affection to the dog (carrying the dog around is a great example), and another, emotional homecomings and departures.

Overcoddling creates a perfect breeding ground for jealousy and separation anxiety, fueled by the violation of sharing den areas. Further, the baby is always sheltered and kept away from the family dog. Yet, to him, prey drive is brought forward due to the similarity of the baby's noise and movement to living prey that he would normally pursue. The possibility of a bite to the child becomes greater and greater as time progresses. I have seen circumstances of just such scenarios taking place, costing all parties involved – a bite to the child, removal of the dog from the home, and the trauma suffered by the family from loss of the dog and physical harm to their child.

Let's move on to emotional homecomings and departures. "It's okay, baby, Mama will be back. It's all right. You be good, now. Mama will see you later." In a word, it's called "separation anxiety." Sometimes, the dog becomes so emotionally dependent upon his owner that he's anxious and timid when out of her presence. He loses all confidence, and canines are meant to be confident and independent. He whines and cries. He becomes hyperactive, pacing and trying to escape. In his frantic attempts, he may cause property damage, such as chewing holes in the walls or carpet. He may even chew on himself out of his great distress. Sometimes, a housebreaking problem will occur with this situation. Ultimately, it creates incredible insecurity in the dog, a feeling much like a panic attack when the owner leaves the house or, in the worst case, the room. Veterinarians have diagnosed this behavior as "separation anxiety." Many prescribe various sedative medications only because they realize that the owners are not willing to change their interaction with the dog.

Another problem resulting from too much love and not enough discipline is lack of respect for the owner. If a dog is shown excessive physical love and praise for no reason, why, then, should he bother to obey when given a command? There is no incentive. After all, if we were constantly praised by our bosses with no effort on our part, our sense of striving to please would diminish until it disappeared. A protracted loss of respect for an owner could ultimately earn him a bite from his own dog.

In the canine world, everything revolves around survival, a basic instinct for promotion. If a dog perceives his owner as weak, allowing him to call the shots in the home, he will step up to bat. If he is put in charge, he will indeed do just that, and put his owner in his place physically at some point in time. This is why leadership is so important.

For now, remember this ancient canine proverb: *If you treat your dog like a human, he will indeed treat you like a dog.*

## *WRONG THING #2: BUT, MY DOG ALWAYS SLEEPS WITH ME!*

It's time to talk about another of the behavior problems **created by** unwitting owners. This problem can have catastrophic results. It is created by allowing your dog to sleep on your furniture and in your beds. Let's consider another aspect of a canine's thinking and instincts, and it has to do with something called a "den." In Chapter One, I discussed what a den is. I also said that canines will defend their den areas violently if necessary. Well, furniture and beds are *your* den areas, but if allowed, a dog will eventually claim them as his own. Further, a dog is not able to make the distinction between jumping on furniture or jumping on a person, meaning that a jumping problem cannot be solved if the dog is allowed to continue sleeping on beds and furniture.

With defending den areas in mind, imagine the following scenario:

Your dog has been allowed to sleep on your den areas for a period of time. Everything seems to be just fine until one day, you drag yourself through the door after a long day at work and attempt to flop on the couch or stretch out across your (and I stress **"your"**) bed. Rover is already occupying that place. You will be utterly shocked to see him stand in a defensive position, teeth bared, growling and barking at you. He is defending his (your) den area. In his mind, it now belongs to him. Well, even though you may be sleeping on the floor that night, you unknowingly allowed this behavior to continue until it became part of your dog's personality. He has claimed your stuff as his own. Is the dog mean? Certainly not; remember, he's a canine. He responds by instinct to certain stimuli and behaviors which have been allowed and deemed acceptable. He doesn't view his violent reaction as anything but normal. In fact, he's wondering what *your* problem is!

This is another behavior problem (and a dangerous one if not properly corrected) that can result in the demise of a perfectly good dog through lack of understanding on our part of the canine nature. He may ultimately take that final trip to the pound not knowing what he did wrong.

A final word to the wise with regard to den areas: Watch the toys you allow your dog to have and *never* allow him to sleep on a cushion or blanket in his kennel. There is always danger to dogs in that they may swallow articles and objects that they cannot expel by normal means. Fabric toys, such as stuffed animals, and cushions to sleep on have one thing in common, and that is "bite sensation." Example: the dog has been chewing his soft cuddlies for some time. The next thing you will see is teeth marks in his cushion, then stuffing pulled out, then, eventually, no more cushion. He walks over to your sofa and sniffs. He tests the biting sensation of *that* cushion and it feels the same. Big hunk out of your sofa! There is no difference in biting sensation; in fact, the sofa is even more wonderful. Oh, boy! It's a BIG stuffed toy! I have seen instances where entire sofas have been demolished right down to the frame and springs while the family was away at work. So, do yourself and your dog a favor and stay away from this practice. Understand furthermore that a pack of dogs will prefer bigger game (i.e. your sofa).

You might wonder what is an acceptable chew toy. Remember that canines have large canine teeth. Nothing fortifies the need to chew more than a traditional dog bone. (A tip here is to avoid rawhide bones. A simple experiment will demonstrate that a small piece of rawhide in a glass of water overnight will expand to several times its size. This means that as this process takes place in your dog's digestive system, he may not be able to pass it. The next step may be surgery.) A traditional, real bone is your best and healthiest choice for your dog.

Let's continue to learn about what not to do with our dogs and explore…

## ***WRONG THING #3: I ALWAYS LEAVE FOOD AND WATER OUT***

Okay, I'll give you a little insight here. Imagine constantly giving your diapered toddler fluid and food, fluid and food, fluid and food....well, you get the picture. Indeed, this will make your potty-training much more difficult. Our canines need to be taught to use a potty spot outside, and they don't have the ability to come to you and say, "Hey, I gotta go!" I can already hear the denial-oriented argument of, "My dog barks or goes to the door to let me know he has to go," or "Why doesn't he let us know?" Remember that we are addressing an existing housebreaking problem, in which case the dog needs to be confined to a kennel and not running loose in the house to go potty whenever and wherever, out of your sight and knowledge. (May I interject here that many people have told me that they leave food and water out and have no problem with housebreaking. I say, they don't *know* they have one. Bring in that special light and go over your carpet one day. Well, maybe you'd rather not, but I did say in the beginning that I was going to be honest with you. Denial doesn't solve issues.)

A dog that continually relieves himself in the house will adopt this act as a practiced behavior, and practice makes perfect, *especially with canines,* who learn almost everything by repetition. They are creatures of habit! This applies to both new puppies and adopted adult canines, the latter of whom may easily develop this problem due to being kept in *constant* confinement in a kennel run or facility. They become used to going in the kennel, gifting you with a housebreaking issue.

The key to this type of problem is twofold. The first is *food and water monitoring.* That is, delegate what is going into your dog's system. Do not free-feed and free-water. This is asking for a problem, especially if you work and are away from home for many hours during the day. For adult dogs, only allow enough water in the morning and no food until evening, when you may give more water *and* take him out several times before you retire and kennel him. Adult canines should only be fed one to two times per day. Get your dog outside as quickly as possible when you arrive home. Take him on his leash and collar to his designated potty spot (using the same area will keep your yard from becoming a minefield and save *you* lots of extra clean-up time). Give him a potty command, such as "Be a good boy (or girl)," and be patient. Be sure to praise him *while he is in the act!* Give lavish verbal praise and act as though you've just won the lottery as he relieves himself. Positive reinforcement is a vital key here. Remember – your dog has an instinctive desire to please you. It works in every scenario, even here.

Also, it's harsh reality time. It is not recommended for people who are away at work all day to begin with an infant puppy. Puppies take much care and monitoring, an impossible goal when you're not there. The ideal situation for raising a puppy is to have a situation where at least one person is home to care for, work with, and monitor the puppy. (Most puppies aged four months or younger will have the need to relieve themselves every two to four hours, and after playing, sleeping, or eating.)

The second key to housebreaking is *utilization of a wire kennel.* The wire kennel allows him to see everything around him, and he will adopt this kennel as his den. Occupying his kennel, or den, also brings into play the survival instinct of a canine, meaning that he will not desire to relieve himself in the same space where he sleeps and eats. Contrary to the opinions of some that dogs are "dirty" animals, they actually insist that their den areas be clean. Though your efforts through these means may *seem* futile, your dog will eventually get the picture.

Finally, never allow your dog to watch you clean his soiled den or other soiled areas. He is still very much a pack animal that can learn from example as well as repetition. In his mind, he sees that Mom or Dad will clean up his mess, so it's okay, and his den (and he) will be clean every day at some point. These methods may seem harsh, but if you want to effectively solve your problem, watch your human reasoning and emotion. Deal with canines as canines, and you will achieve your desired result.


## *WRONG THING #4: MY DOG LOVES TUG-OF-WAR*


It's the ultimate game to play with the family dog. It's how we see fathers and sons interact with their dogs on television all the time. It's considered wholesome, all-American fun, but can quickly develop into a clear and present danger to all who may encounter it. As a canine behaviorist for many years, I haven't seen a problem with an aggressive dog yet that this harmful practice didn't have something to do with at some point in the dog's conditioning. Granted, you just didn't know. But, you do now.

The typical puppy learns at an early age how to roughhouse and mouth. This is quite natural behavior as it builds confidence, endurance, and drive. However, it is the family that pays the biggest penalty because this becomes a behavior for the puppy. By the time he reaches the four-month-old stage, it is part of his personality.

Tug-of-war brings into practice some dangerous instincts in your dog. Getting back to the canine mind for a moment, remember what was shared about pack issues? The need for promotion was one of them. In the wild, this is perfectly normal and, I might add, necessary for survival. However, your home is not a wilderness and your dog must learn what is acceptable and what is not. Playing tug-of-war allows your dog to express aggressive drive, such as growling, barking, and trying to win that rope or piece of cloth from you, his owner. If he gets a winner, he has just been promoted. What does that mean to his status versus yours in the pack at that point? Remember, he's won. His attitude is one of pride – "I beat you! I beat you!" He will not forget that. Keep in mind as well that whatever he does, he is practicing for "the big one." Just as a fighter trains tirelessly, working out at the gym, running, sparring, and getting his body physically ready, so is your dog. If the game is played over and over, you are unknowingly creating a dangerous dog. In fact, I stated earlier that dogs learn by repetition, and he is learning repeatedly to try to win. He will, by nature, turn up the juices, and someone could get hurt. This is especially dangerous with larger breeds who become huge adult canines. I have seen countless dogs given up by their owners as "aggressive," when the problem was actually created and encouraged by this practice. I might add here that some police canines are professionally trained and conditioned for bite work in just this way.

Another natural instinct that tug-of-war lifts to ultimate levels is something called *"prey drive."* "Prey" itself is an animal taken for food by another animal.

Simply put, "prey drive" is the desire to hunt or chase. Although basic to a canine's survival in the wild, your dog is not existing in the wild, but within your family scenario. Fanning the flames of prey drive *from* the owner *to* his dog is very dangerous. If you have allowed this practice, I recommend that children should not be left unattended with the dog. Children like to run and, in many cases, a dog conditioned by tug-of-war and roughhouse games will view them as moving prey.

One final word on a related topic here is bite levels. Just as repetitive displays of aggression allowed in tug-of-war increase the danger level to the owner, the same is true in a situation where the family dog has already gotten a winning bite on a family member. It always begins with a gentle mouthing on a weak member of the family, such as a small child. Gradually, the intensity of the bite increases. They are called "blood bites," and they progress in upward levels. The next level is a puncture wound, the next draws real blood and requires stitches, and the final level is the ultimate one, where the dog clamps on and shakes, causing a maiming or worse. Further, after winning bites on weaker pack (family) members, a canine will continue his natural drive for promotion by moving on to the pack member next in the hierarchy level, which is usually Mom, if she does not understand her dog's nature and considers him her baby. His ultimate goal is simply "top dog." That phrase, though lightly used, means just exactly that, and is derived from life within a pack of dogs. We discussed leadership values earlier, and this is a prime reason why you want to maintain yours. Any attempt by your dog to mouth on you or any member of your family is the ultimate no-no, and must be dealt with instantly and radically. Scruffing is the method of choice, among other distracting means, but dominance must be firmly established first, and its application must be taught. Scruffing was discussed in Chapter One, and is the method used by a dog's own mother for correction within the pack. However, our application is not anywhere near as violent as hers would be! A scruff correction is a quick taking down of the dog by his scruff, or back of his neck, then letting go. Timing is everything on this – you must catch him in the act and correct immediately so that he will know what behavior he is being corrected for. In cases where the owner is unfamiliar with this method and has no leadership or dominance over his dog, it is my best recommendation that a canine training professional who deals with aggressors be consulted.

If aggression is directed to immediate family members, removing the dog from your family environment is the best recommendation as aggression cannot be guaranteed not to resurface.

## *WRONG THING #5: MY DOG IS CRAZY ABOUT ENCHILADAS!*

Table food. Fine for you. Wrong for Mr. Canine. There are excellent dog foods on the market specifically designed to help your dog's body function to its ultimate health capacity. As is the case with all the other wrong things we do to our dogs, it comes down to our own unwitting selfishness – it makes us feel gratified to give our dogs something we believe is good. In the case of table food, I can tell you this - it causes health problems for dogs along with all of the other unhealthy consequences it bestows on us, such as clogged arteries and the like. Your dog's physiological needs are different than yours, and it is your responsibility to keep him as healthy as possible.

A more serious health issue with table food is tooth decay. We have the ability to brush our teeth; our dogs don't. I've heard the arguments from people who have their dogs' teeth brushed, but I maintain that table food is an unhealthy thing for a dog. It may gratify you to share your cheeseburger with your dog, but after years of a human diet and the damage it causes to your dog's teeth, you will wonder why, one day, he suddenly "snapped" and delivered a serious bite. A toothache is never fun, and no one likes to be toyed with in any form or fashion when they have one. However, the dog may pay the price with his life by being removed from the home as being unpredictable and vicious when the problem was created by the owner.

## *WRONG THING #6: I HIT MY DOG WHEN HE DOES WRONG*

Hitting is a human reaction which is totally detrimental to interacting with your dog, for he cannot understand the overall message being given. Therefore, instead of making the connection between being hit and what he has done wrong, he instead establishes a fear of forward body movements. He does not learn that his behavior is unacceptable; he learns to never get caught at it. Although I don't believe a reader of this book physically abuses his or her dog, let me just interject a word of warning about this practice. If physically abused, a dog will begin to believe that he must become defensive. This produces a canine which does not have a lot of confidence, and he may begin to show some form of aggression. In such a case, the owner has to have a firm understanding that the idea is to instill confidence, not fear.

While I am on the subject, let's discuss the ultimate denial about dogs…

## <u>*WORST WRONG THING: MY DOG DOESN'T BITE*</u>

Has your dog bitten before? Has it been "someone he didn't like," the meter reader, or the mailman? If this has occurred, do not assume that because he doesn't bite *you,* he'll never bite at all or, perhaps, again. I have heard a variety of excuses, and that is exactly what they are, for why someone's dog bit another person. Please do not ever excuse this behavior to defend your dog. Biting a human being is completely unacceptable for your dog, who is a family member. Remember, too, the previous discussion related to increasing levels of bites. A bite is a winner. The need for promotion comes into play. There have also been many instances where a dog who only bit for this reason or that reason finally did end up tagging the owner in denial – a brutal awakening. Without knowledge of canine thinking and behavior, the unwitting owner is not only physically hurt by the dog, but left confused, angry, and disappointed. After all, he only tried to make the dog happy, fed him, paid vet bills, and on and on.

Proper conditioning from the start will avoid this problem from ever getting started. Let me share with you a few things you can do as a responsible and caring owner to prevent aggressive behavior in your dog.

Isolation is a prime cause for the development of aggression in canines. In this situation, a dog is placed in an environment where he cannot interact with or view family members or territory (your home). Here are a few examples:

1) Locked in the garage;
2) Confined to one room of the house, looking at four walls all day;
3) Confined in a dark basement;
4) Attached to a tree in the yard.

All of these situations create sensory deprivation. Silence is torment for a dog's delicate and very advanced sense of hearing. Imagine yourself in his situation, alone for eight hours or more without social interaction, without much light, without much sound, not knowing when you will be free again. The punishment of isolation in humans creates dementia. Imagine how your dog feels and the type of behavior he will exhibit upon release. Excessive exuberance is one – jumping, barking, hyperactive running, and pushing. The other is aggression. You can create a "Cujo" in your dog by isolating him.

Specifically, number four above is the worst scenario in isolation. A dog on a chain is the most common of canine aggressors. He is left outside to deal with the elements, teased, hurt (and sometimes killed) by outsiders, and more than likely physically abused by his owners. His survival instinct is in high gear. If your dog is on a tie-down outside, discontinue this practice. When training on a leash and collar begins, he may be immune to leash correction simply from constantly straining at his chain or other tie-down mechanism outside.

In closing, please know that aggression cannot be proofed. Although the implementation of behavior modification is extremely effective for other problems, aggression is not one of them. I reiterate that if your dog is aggressive, please seek the help of a canine professional. If the dog is aggressive to you or to any family member, removal from the home is your only answer. Not only will you save yourself, your family, and other innocent people from being hurt, there is the costly issue of personal liability for dog bites. More on that later.

## *OKAY, I'M CONVINCED!*

You've learned a lot about canines, which is essential to training. Now, you're ready to learn the training process. Please bear in mind that training increases your dog's confidence, intelligence, spirit, and judge of character. Understand, too, that training is not a two- or three-week experience; it is a way of life for you and your dog. You will recall I said earlier that dogs learn by repetition, so it stands to reason that if you have a dog who jumps and chews constantly without correction, he will be a pro at these practices. If, on the other hand, he learns all of the right things from you and practices daily *as a way of life,* he consistently does the right thing daily.

It's time for another warning for the serious student: Don't ever let up on your teaching. Increasing your dog's confidence and intelligence and then letting the entire process slide will result in behavior problems returning to haunt you tenfold. It's one thing to have a jumper and chewer, but a quite another to have a more *confident, smarter* jumper and chewer. Let's not go there. We're talking about a difference between chewing up the afghan and munching on the auto upholstery. The repetition of training daily keeps you safe.

If you've made it this far, I believe you're serious and desire serious change, so let's get started.

# CHAPTER 4:
# LET'S GET STARTED

## *INTRODUCTION TO TRAINING*

There are five areas to be discussed before we move into actual obedience exercises. You need this input to see the reasons why you will be doing what you're doing in order to achieve your desired result. These areas consist of leadership, timing, consistency, patience, and control.

## *Leadership*

You already are aware by now that you must lead your dog, not the other way around. He learns to trust you, rely upon your judgment, and ultimately obey you when your leadership values are firmly in place on a daily basis throughout his lifetime. Here are some ways to establish leadership in your everyday interaction with your dog:

1. Do not allow the dog to enter or exit before you. It's your world. He waits until he gets the "okay" from you. This also applies to stairs.

2. Avoid games that encourage the dog to display aggression toward his owner, such as tug-of-war or wrestling.

3. Make your dog move if he is in the way. Don't walk around him; don't step over him. He values his space as a vital necessity; so should you. Simply tell him, "Move!" and continue walking, moving him out of the way as you

step. Do this as a practice, just because.

4. Make solid eye contact with your dog when giving commands or corrections, making sure he looks away first. Solid eye contact has a world of meaning to a canine that we, as humans, don't understand. It means inflicting our wills.

***\* Only Exception: Please remember the following instruction when encountering an <u>unfamiliar dog</u>: Never make solid eye contact. It's a direct challenge and can get you hurt. It is vitally important to teach children this rule. \****

Along with solid eye contact comes an attitude called "intent." You want it done. You want it done now. There are no exceptions or excuses. As your training advances, your dog will correct himself simply by observing the combination of intent with solid eye contact. A great example of this is derived from the experience of baby boomers. Get a picture of this: Child is in the living room cutting up. Dad is in the chair reading the newspaper. Dad gives one verbal warning, which is blown off by the child. The next time, Dad doesn't say a word. He simply *lowers the newspaper, looking directly at that child with unmistakable INTENT.* Child stops cutting up.

5. Tell your dog when it is okay to begin eating. Do not allow him to eat at leisure. This is Leadership 101. You are his food source, after all. Give him an allotted amount of time to finish (15 to 20 minutes). Pick the bowl up until the next feeding.

6. Do not share your den areas, such as bed and furniture. As discussed previously, this is a dangerous practice and results in an immediate loss of leadership. It puts you in the position of sibling rather than leader.

## *<u>Timing</u>*

Never correct in the aftermath. Correcting your dog after the fact only confuses him and creates stress. You need to solve his unwanted behavior by catching him in the act. In addition, the way in which you correct your dog in the process of unwanted behavior is vital. NEVER HIT YOUR DOG! This is a human reaction which the dog cannot associate with his behavior, but with you. In other words, the behavior is okay; just don't get caught. Hitting also causes him to be what we call "hand-shy," or afraid of forward body movements. How a canine reacts to repeated hitting varies on temperament and conditioning. He may become a cowering bundle of nerves, or he may defend himself and strike back. Stay away from this practice.

## *Consistency*

The canine, in most instances, is a conditioned animal. He will learn by repetition.

We discussed pecking orders earlier. It's important as you begin training. He must know his ranking, which is follower and not leader. Every family member must practice the same things the same way. There are no exceptions to this rule. Practice makes perfect, and you need to be patient enough to wait for the results you are looking for. When children are present in the home, they and other family members must know what is acceptable behavior (theirs and the dog's) and what is not. It defeats the purpose of training if other people or animals are allowed to encourage unacceptable behavior. Let me give you examples of these situations.

Situation One: You have been rigorously practicing your training exercises and know that it is of vital importance not to give affection, petting, etc., to your dog unless he does something for it. The most effective trainers teach with *positive reinforcement,* teaching the dog that if he desires your hand petting him, he must perform, or obey a given command, in order to receive what he wants. If you ignore this rule, as pointed out earlier, you'll be constantly loving on the dog and wondering why he blows you off when you call him to come or heel. Why should he? You'll pet him anyway, usually excessively and for no reason at all.

We need to interject at this point another after-effect of overcoddling. In many of my group obedience meetings, it is easy to see those who pet their dogs excessively and inadvertently at home. Whenever a dog performs correctly, these individuals forget to give him a pet and a "Good dog!" at that crucial time, positively reinforcing that the dog did well and deserves praise. Why do they forget? They get into such a habit of petting the dog for no reason that they have forgotten what the method of positive reinforcement is all about. (Just as a reminder as you begin your training.)

Unknown to most people, most professional dog trainers are very strict in regard to interacting with their dogs, and are always aware of the behavior they do and do not want to be encouraged. If the dog is allowed to jump on that person or mouth on that person, it's setback time! It's called inconsistency. If allowed to continue, this dog will soon be jumping on everyone who walks in the door, or you'll spend too much time correcting him for this behavior and will be constantly frustrated. (At this juncture, you may actually be changing his name from "Fido" to "No".) What will happen in this scenario is that, although your dog will obey *you,* the person who insists upon overcoddling the dog will be ignored by the dog. He or she will not be respected or even treated very nicely by Mr. Canine. The person with the too-willing hand will eventually find himself trying to continue to *like* the dog. I have encountered situations in homes where, for example, the lady of the house refuses to comply with the rule regarding overcoddling. She pets the dog all the time. Husband comes home and dog wears a halo for him. He obeys every command, keeps his attention on that man, and shows the utmost respect. Wife, however, begins to experience the infliction of the dog's will by way of mouthing, pushing, defiance, or worse. To the wife, the dog soon becomes "that #@*&! dog", and finally, "YOUR @$#*&! dog."

Situation Two: I mentioned other animals being allowed to encourage bad behavior, and you might be wondering how this is possible. If Uncle Billy Bob brings over his hyperactive, undisciplined dog, who is allowed to jump on people and furniture, nose into the trash can, and chase the kids around the house, well… monkey see, monkey do. It's as simple as that.

On this subject, I need to also add that it is probably not advisable to allow your dog to "play" with other dogs. What we see as playing is actually increasing the dog's drive and improving his skills, whether we want to believe it or not. Remember, we are dealing with the *canine mind* and not our own. Also in this regard, allowing this practice can ultimately get your dog hurt in a situation where he runs up to "play" with an unfamiliar dog who simply doesn't play. Rover gets his nose rearranged, or worse. So, follow the rules and keep your dog safe by understanding who and what he actually is.

Keep the rules of training and interaction within your circle of family and friends very, very clear. Remember that you are the dog's trainer and guardian, which makes you responsible for his/her actions. Why bother to train if you must go back and try to fix regressive behavior on a daily basis? It is not fair to you and, especially, not to your dog.

## *Patience*

You must not be angry when interacting with your dog during training - rather, be firm. Your dog will detect anger and frustration and will react. It is important to have realistic expectations. Every dog has a different personality and temperament. (The huge advantage of training is that it takes weeks to teach your dog and years to teach humans!)

The only exception to daily training is if you are having an exceptionally bad day. The reason I interjected "exceptionally" is because it would be very easy to have every day be a bad day. Let's face it, life can be way too stressful. However, achieving those awesome results with your dog takes time and effort. As you train, do not expect him to do well. Why? If you expect to have to correct your dog, you will experience much less disappointment. Instead, adopt the attitude of: "Go ahead and mess up so I can correct and teach. Then, we'll continue to progress." This positive attitude actually helps both of you during the initial process. You will correct and praise according to results rather than expecting your dog to reason as you do and "just get it." He will, believe me.

## *Control*

As a dog owner, you have the power of changing environments, scheduling feeding times, creating the scenarios to solve various behavior problems, and leading your dog. It does no good to have a trainer train your dog. Instead, you need the insight into who and what he is, how he thinks, why he behaves the way he does, how to interact with him properly and consistently, and the way to control him yourself.

## **LANGUAGE IN TRAINING**

There are three tones of voice in training, and you must be very aware of your tone during this process. You can communicate your seriousness and intent with a ***command tone,*** pleasure with his performance (or encouraging in the process of training) with a ***praising tone,*** or stern and definite with a ***correction tone.*** Understanding and using the proper tone will complement your handling methods and clearly convey your wishes on a level that your dog can understand. Effective verbal communication between you and your dog is a vital tool in achieving the goals of obedience training. Clearly, a frustrated, upset tone conveys confusion to your dog. This is why your training must be to the point and bereft of human emotion. He will not respond to anger or frustration; he picks up on it, but cannot understand. Therefore, you will not get a response; you will have a war with the leash and the dog.

## *PRAISE*

When Rover obeys, he must be rewarded. Positive reinforcement, or working for "good dog," is never done with treats. If your dog learns that his reward is edible rather than a loving touch from you, you have created a bad situation for yourself. If you are outside, in a scenario where it is vital that your dog obey, and you discover you've forgotten to put treats in your pocket, you're out of luck. What if you run out of treats? What about when he's no longer hungry or interested in them? Constantly rewarding with treats is also detrimental to your dog's health, as you will soon have an overweight dog with those attendant problems, not to mention dental concerns. Also, you can create a housebreaking problem because of the very fact that you are overloading his tummy.

On the other hand, the correct praise is your pleased tone of voice, facial expression, and petting on the chest. The reason I prefer petting the chest rather than the head is that some dogs become overstimulated by hands in their faces. They will become overly excited and think the whole thing is over. They may also become annoyed with hands before their eyes – in their space. Try it sometime to test this theory. Simply walk up to someone (whom you know will still like you afterward!) and pet him in the face repeatedly. Tousle his hair, tweak his ears, and rub his chin. Our instant reaction is annoyance and the need to back away from the intruding hands. Your dog feels the same way.

You will quickly discover how much praise is too much, especially with puppies. When you see overstimulation, try petting briefly on the chest. For some dogs, using verbal praise with no petting works best. This method still reinforces that he has performed well, but keeps the stimulation to a minimum.

## *CORRECTION*

We have been discussing throughout the introduction to training how to properly correct your dog and the things that you do not do. You may wonder, "What is the *proper* correction in training?" The answer is in leash correction, tone, attitude, and eye contact. As I explain the different training exercises, I will give an example of proper leash correction for the instances when your dog does not obey and, especially, when he is first learning the process. The leash correction in one instance is not always the same in another. Leash correction is always accompanied by a distinct "No!"

Tone, attitude and eye contact is the trifecta of correction that, when used correctly, can get results as quickly and effectively as physical corrections. This is true for a dog who knows what is expected of him/her, but is being stubborn.

## *TRAINING TIPS:*

1) **Consistency pays!** In training, always use the same words for the same ideas. For example, if you want to teach "down," don't say, "lie down" one time, and "down, boy" the next time. Keep the commands short, but most of all, make them exactly the same every time. The same applies to hand signals. Be sure you are using the proper hand, leading with the proper foot, etc.

2) **Introduce commands slowly,** only after your dog has performed the behavior you want spontaneously. You wait, he sits. His reward for this is "Good sit!" from you. In this way, your dog learns to associate the word and action with pleasure, the only real combination in training a dog to do anything.

3) ***Make training sessions pleasurable for all involved.*** This doesn't mean that you shouldn't be serious about your training. You should, but be pleasant and firm. The only taboo is laughing at the dog during training, which will only humiliate him or turn him into a clown.

4) ***Keep sessions short, especially at first.*** Start with a 10-15 minute session and work your way up. This is for your sanity as well! It also ensures that your effort will not be wasted. Remember as you progress, however, that the more time spent in training results in bigger and better rewards.

5) ***Patience, patience, patience!*** Not that your dog is a slow learner; nothing could be further from the truth. Yet, most people are unreasonable in their expectations. If your attitude is, "Let's get started and see what happens," you'll be rewarded in the short run by a more pleasant session each time out. The long haul? Much better-trained dog. Also, keeping patience in mind causes you to remember not to allow yourself to become frustrated. Frustration will accomplish nothing in training. Your dog will pick up on that and mirror with his lack of behavior exactly what he's sensing from you. Back to that sanity issue again.

6) ***End each session before you both tire of it.*** If you feel yourself getting short-tempered, stop there even if you've only been at it for five minutes. (Did I mention a sanity issue?)

7) ***Use praise as a reward rather than food.*** A dog performs for food only if it is purposely starved, which will hardly make him look forward to the sessions. Dogs will do for your approval what they would never consider for a bite to eat as long as it is made worth it.

8) ***Be firm with both your dog and yourself.*** If you pay attention to what you're doing, praising and rewarding the exact response you want, the dog will learn it correctly after a few times. If you are inattentive, the work gets tougher. Between sessions, reward the behavior whenever you see it, but don't be fanatical or overdo it. If your canine is led to expect praise when he performs properly, he will become disappointed on the inevitable occasion that you seemed to have missed. This reinforces your teaching!

9) ***Never punish.*** Rather than punishing, which is a concept a dog does not understand, you must arrange for an unpleasant consequence to clue the dog when he misbehaves. This is entirely different from punishment (a human response which plays with emotions) and much better for the purpose of training. It is simple and straightforward; he associates his behavior with the consequence he ended up with, not with you. With regard to your leash in teaching obedience modification, correction is vital or your dog will not learn what he is expected to do. The better he becomes at obedience, the

less leash correction will be necessary, until he has reached the sought-after state of off-leash.

10. ***Use your dog's name as part of moving commands.*** Command with, "Charlie, heel!" There is no more pleasant sound than that of one's own name.

11. ***When you first start training, practice in the same place every day, and be sure there are no distractions.*** This is the one reason a training class is not the ideal place for real training, especially for beginners. After your dog has learned his lessons, you can then begin to work in other surroundings so that he will become accustomed to obey in all conditions, including with the distractions of noise, traffic, people, and other animals.

12. ***Never grab at your dog or chase after him.*** Of course, your leash is the reason you will never have to chase Rover down the block. Chasing or swinging at your dog causes him to become hand-shy and almost impossible to handle.

13. ***Vary your tones with the appropriate words.*** Praise, of course, is given in a warm, friendly tone. It is not what you say that is most important to your dog, but *the way you say it!* When a dog is new to an experience, coax him along. Later, it can be expected for the dog to understand, and you must use a command tone. This is a tone that demands obedience. Your dog is a lot better at recognizing a shift in tones than you are. Avoid the irritable, crabby voice of whining. Commands are to be given as such, so a questioning tone such as "Rover…sit?" is as effective in commanding your dog as it would be for a drill sergeant in the military to politely inquire whether his troop would like to move out. A questioning tone creates uncertainty in your dog. Should he sit or not? He wonders whether *you're* sure you want him to sit. Review the section on "Language in Training."

14. ***Be sure your dog is in the same happy mental state when you end the session as when you started.*** The simplest way to do this is to be sure your frame of mind is good. If you are still up and full of enthusiasm, your dog will be as well.

15. ***Remember that commanding and sharp corrections go hand in hand.*** The *reward* (praise) is for what you want to *encourage*. Don't bother to discourage unwanted behavior if you don't have the proper timing on corrections. For example, if your dog jumps on you, never stand there and repeat, "Down!" "No!" Use that leash with a sharp "Off!" Let that be that. He'll learn a lot faster. The "down" command in training means to down on all fours. "Off" means to get off you, the chair, Aunt Bea….right now.

# *YOUR TWO OBJECTIVES*

Training has two essential classifications: *Obedience Modification* and *Behavior Modification.* In order to avoid information overload, let's begin with obedience modification, including training exercises, and then move on to behavior modification.

**Obedience modification** is the teaching of verbal (and later, non-verbal, using hand signals only) commands. These commands are as follows:

1) **COME:** The "come" command is the most important to teach your dog. He must learn to come to you at all times, under any circumstance, even if he has done wrong. This command must always be given in a pleasant tone. Never reprimand your dog on a come command, no matter what he has done, or he will learn to be afraid to come to you. This is one command that could save your life or his.

2) **SIT:** Well, this is self-explanatory. However, your dog will learn to sit directly before you after he has come to you, or sit any time he is told to do so.

3) **WAIT:** The **wait** command means your dog must freeze in motion if moving, or wait while sitting, until you give him the "okay" or another command. This command is a lifesaver to your dog. It can prevent him from being hit by a car or from being hurt by any other life-threatening situation. This is the most critical command for your dog's safety.

4) **HEEL:** The **heel** command is the one in which your dog learns to walk with you.

23

5) **RETURN-TO-HEEL:** The **return-to-heel** command places your dog in a position to walk with you. There are three of these commands, called **direct, side, and facing.** These will be discussed in detail as we move on to teaching the obedience exercises. Although the exercise is to teach the dog to return to proper positioning, the command for all three returns is still simply "heel," rather than "Return to heel."

6) **DOWN:** The **down** command drops your dog down on all fours from any position.

7) **RETURN-TO-SIT:** The **return-to-sit** command is simply returning your dog from a down position to a sit position.

As training advances, these commands will be combined:

Come *and sit;*
Come, then *wait* (freeze in motion) while in progress toward you;

Sit and *wait;*
Heel, then *wait* while in progress;
Heel, then *down* while in progress (referred to as "walk/downs");
Heel, then *sit* while in progress (referred to as "walk/sits");

Down and *return-to-sit* (called "yo-yo's");

## *EQUIPMENT YOU WILL NEED*

To begin your training, you must have three vital pieces of equipment:

1) Properly-sized, nylon slip collar. (I recommend a collar that is braided and stitched rather than glued, as they are much sturdier and hold up well.)

2) Six-foot by one-inch nylon or leather training leash;

3) Wire kennel proportionate to his size and future growth.

4) A good, positive attitude!

Leash control is everything in this process. Please do not attempt training exercises without one. Your leash is your control mechanism (along with positive reinforcement). If you give a command and are not in a position to reinforce it, you have just been blown off. Once your basic obedience training has been perfected, you will begin advanced training and gearing your dog toward off-leash. This is why he must be perfect *on* a leash before he can be trusted to be *off* one. Leash laws may vary from state to state. Please pay close attention to your local and state ordinances.

Keep your training time to a minimum of 15 to 20 minutes per session, per person, daily. Of course, the more you work with him, the better and quicker your results. Some of my best students began even their initial training time at one to two hours. (I do not advise this length with puppies, however, because of their lack of attention span.) Adult dogs will thrive with this daily work ethic, and believe it or not, they like to work! Canines have a working mentality by nature. It's unrealistic and unfair to expect your dog to simply hang around for the duration of his life. Give him a purpose and reason for being, remembering that he has a natural desire to please you, his owner.

Please discontinue your session for the day if you become frustrated or angry. How many people do you know who can learn anything from an angry teacher? Look forward to your sessions with your dog! Have fun with the process of teaching and watching his progress. Handle with confidence!

## *Lesson #1 – COME*

To begin teaching this most essential command, we will combine it with the "sit" command, as the proper "come" is always followed by a "sit." Begin on one knee with your dog out at six feet of leash in front of you. Especially in cases where you are teaching a puppy, being more on his height enhances a feeling of security and that it's all right to proceed toward you. (A six-foot-two-inch man standing before a puppy is intimidating to the little guy, to say the least.) Making sure your tone is pleasant and encouraging, bring either arm in a sweeping motion to your chest, use his name first, and tell him to "come." When properly learned, he will come directly in front of you and sit, looking up at you for his next command. However, in the beginning, this obviously will not happen. If he overshoots you, goes to either side, or simply doesn't know *what* to do, begin backing up and gently bringing him toward you with your leash. The reason for backing up is to teach him to work to get to you.

Your leash control will be as follows (and for the sake of simplicity, I will illustrate as for a right-handed person):

a) With your right hand grasping your end of the leash, your thumb in the loop, open your left hand, palm up, and slide the leash toward you, all the way until your hand makes contact with the clasp around your dog's neck.

b) Upon contact with the clasp with your left hand, your right hand and arm will be free. Drop the leash from your right hand and, using a scooping upward motion with that hand, tell him to "sit."

Be sure to praise him when he begins to get it. Diligent repetition is necessary, especially with puppies.

Your non-verbal command for "come" is either arm to the chest in a wide, sweeping arc.

## *Lesson #2 – SIT*

This will be one of your easier training exercises. Use both a verbal command of "sit" with the corresponding hand signal as explained in Lesson #1, right hand scooping upward. If needed, correct the dog with a firm jerk on the lead. If you can get the head to go up, the rear goes down. Don't forget to praise!

## *Lesson #3 – WAIT*

Whenever this command is given, place your hand over your dog's eyes for a brief moment and tell him, "Wait." The reason for the hand over his eyes is that it creates a momentary blackout of his visual field, reinforcing the fact that he must not move forward. It is important to remember that the wait command is vital and the tone used when giving it must be firm.

After telling your dog to wait verbally and with the corresponding hand signal, be sure to always step out away from him with your **right** foot. He will pick up left and right very quickly, and stepping out with your left leg will be his sign to begin heeling with you. Your dog will teach you consistency in this area once he learns this. You may find yourself wondering why he won't wait on command, not realizing that you're giving him a double message - telling him to wait and then stepping out with your left foot.

The wait command is also used in another, more advanced exercise, which you will not be ready to begin until your basic obedience has been completed. This exercise is called "waiting at the curb." On this one, your tone is everything. You will be commanding your dog to freeze at the curb before moving out into the street and, possibly, the path of a car. Your tone should be the same as if you were freezing your child from the same situation. If you can imagine how you would sound in that situation, that is the tone needed when teaching waiting at curbs or utilizing the wait command in a potentially dangerous situation.

Your non-verbal command for "wait" at a distance is simply either hand extended fully out from your body, palm facing away, fingers pointing up.

## *Lesson #4 – Heel*

The basic heel command is to teach your dog how to walk with you. His position should always be on your left side, head parallel to your knee, and slightly behind your left leg. With your verbal command of "heel," your hand signal is to slap your left thigh at the same time as the command is given, then take off with your left foot first. Remember that if you step out with your right foot first after your dog has learned how to heel, he will not move with you. He will be watching which foot you lead with; that will always be his cue.

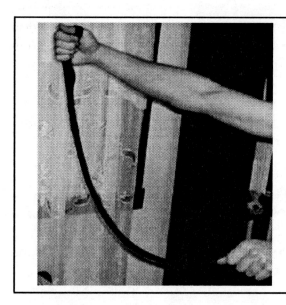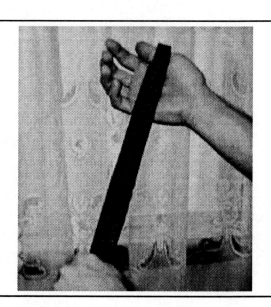

Your leash control while heeling is called a "cuff." Slide your right thumb through the loop, then take up approximately half of the leash length, wrapping it over the looped thumb. Your left hand will be responsible for the remaining length of leash. This hand should not be tightly closed on the leash. Rather, let the leash slide freely between your left thumb and index finger. Most of your actual control will be done with your right hand.

While you and your dog are walking together, do not allow him to:

1) Cross in front of your path. If this occurs, tell him "no," while pulling back sharply on the leash in your left hand. This moves your dog back into proper positioning. Another correction for this is to turn a sharp left directly in front of him and keep moving.

2) Strain forward and pull *you*! Your dog should never be allowed to lead you anywhere. His place is on your left side, walking at your pace. If he begins to pull you forward on lead, make an abrupt, very tight change of direction back the way you came. Your leash control while doing this is to drop the cuff in your right hand, but keep your thumb in the loop. Your left hand will still be in the same position. Your dog will soon be out at six feet of leash behind you, doing his own thing. Give the leash a meaningful jerk with your

right hand, telling him to "Hurry!" and keeping your left hand sliding through the leash as he catches up with you. Use verbal praise when he catches up.

Any time your dog wants to go north, you turn sharply and proceed south. Don't watch to see what he does, or wait for him to catch up. Just *move!* Adopt a "places to go, people to see" attitude. The reason for this is to teach your dog that he will pay a price for pulling and not heeling properly. All he will see is your back moving in another direction, and he must hurry to catch up. Remember to praise as he does catch up, without breaking stride in your movements.

3) Refuse to move with you. Just go! Give your verbal and hand signals, get that left foot out there and start stepping. Jerk the leash forward with your right thumb while you tell him to "hurry."

4) Veer off in another direction, following his own nose. Of course, this could only be off to the left, as we previously discussed the correction for not allowing him to cross in front of you. If he veers off leftward, tell him "no!" (like you mean it) and use right-hand leash correction to get him back to your left side, as you continue walking. Do not stop and deal with this, just keep walking, letting your leash correction deal with it. (Helpful tip: A good correction for a dog who veers off on a heel is to practice many left turns – turning sharply left right in front of him, stepping in his space, with the command of "Over," which means "left.")

Your entire attitude on a heel is, "Places to go, things to do. I have purpose and intent." This is why I instruct that you not stop your heel to correct problems. Perform these corrections as often as necessary in order to perfect your dog's heel. It is terribly frustrating to have your dog walk you, or veer off in other directions. Taking the time to work through the kinks on your heel exercises will be of great benefit!

## *Lesson #5 – Return-to-Heel*

There are three return-to-heel exercises, also known as "recalls."

1) Direct: Your dog is on a wait. You move out with your right foot first, at six feet of leash out in front of him. Pat your left thigh and call him to "heel." Slide the leash through your left hand, as usual. Your dog's job is to walk up and sit on your left side. Tell him verbally and with the proper hand signal to "sit."

2) Side: With your dog on your right side, pat your left thigh and tell him to

"heel." He is to walk behind you and sit on your left side. Your leash control begins as always, then you must pass the leash behind you as your dog is en route, and then take up the initial leash position, with right thumb through the loop and left hand loosely holding the slack.

3) Facing: With your dog out in front of you at six feet of leash, take your right foot back first. Call him to "heel," slapping your left thigh. Again, your dog must take the path toward you, then around your right side and behind you, ending up sitting on your left side. As he begins moving forward, slide the leash toward you, taking your left foot up to your right foot's position *at the point when your dog passes behind you*, passing the leash behind you as well, and ending up once again with your right thumb through the loop as usual. The reason for taking your right foot back is to help with proper positioning and to help you get your dog there without fighting him pound-for-pound. Very basically, it's leverage.

As your dog learns these three return-to-heel commands, begin by utilizing walls and counters in your home so that he learns exactly where he should be in relation to his eventual sit. For example, on any return-to-heel, he is not to be on your left side, six feet away from you. He should be in tight to your left side, but not invading your space by touching you, leaning against you, or stepping on your foot with his paw. (If he steps on or leans against you, nudge him over to the left with your left leg, telling him "Over".) Using walls and counters, gauge the amount of space he will need to get into this position, leaving him just enough room to squeeze in. That way, when you are working long line (a 20', 30', or 40' leash) and no leash at all, you won't have the problem of him returning to heel at your left side six blocks away!

## *Lesson #6 – Down*

"Down" is a dominance command. No dog likes to "down" simply because he is more confident and secure sitting or on all fours, ready to handle any given situation. Dominant dogs, especially, don't like to "down".

Before practicing downs, begin with a training exercise called "dominance rolls." Place your dog on his back, one hand on his chest to hold him there, and gently go about the business of doing anything a two-year-old might do. In other words, be annoying. Gently take his muzzle (a lip) and move it. Pull his tail gently. Move his paws one by one. Gently pull his ears. I emphasize "gentle" because I don't want to be misunderstood that this is a time to be cruel. Dominance rolls desensitize your dog for handling by veterinarians, groomers, and the unexpected hands-on visit by a child. He gets used to this behavior and learns to not react by biting. During this exercise, be sure to only hold him down by his chest, not pet him. Any dog will lie down for you if you pet his tummy. What you are actually practicing here is dominance, having him expose all his vital organs to you and not allowing him up until you say so. This is a huge trust factor for your dog. It also builds a bond between the two of you. He will give this up because he learns to trust you with everything that makes him tick. Five minutes is usually enough for this exercise.

If mouthing occurs during this process, scruff him. What I mean by this is that you take him by the scruff of his neck (the loose skin at the back of his neck) and pull his head down to the floor quickly. (This was earlier described in Chapter One in relation to his mother's scruff correction.) Timing on this correction is essential. You must look for the mouthing signs, then grab the scruff. If you have a puppy, hold him to the floor by the scruff, making solid eye contact and telling him "No!" He must look away first. If you have an adult dog, make your scruff quick; then it's over with – down to the floor and let go, also with a verbal correction of "No!"

Dominance rolls are excellent for puppies. They stop the mouthing problem before it gets started and establish your leadership from the beginning. Practice this exercise daily for five minutes.

I must caution, however, that if you are working with an adopted adult canine (whose history is unknown - you don't know what his reaction will be) or a dominant or aggressive adult, please seek the assistance of a professional trainer before attempting this exercise.

The actual "down" command is given thus: With leash in hand, place your left hand on the clasp with the command of "down," which must be given firmly, not wavering in tone. As you press down on the clasp, go down on one knee with him in the beginning. This is a less threatening posture to the dog. Take him down, not over. If he tries to get up, don't tell him to "down" again. Simply tell him "No!" and use your leash correction. If he persists in popping up, utilize your left foot on the clasp until he downs. If he struggles or resists, simply keep your foot on the leash. He will ultimately make the decision to down because it will be physically easier for him to lie down rather than fight the resistance of the leash.

If you have persistent problems with downing, put him on a sit-and-wait for a longer period of time, putting him back into the sit position with your leash correction if he tries to down (which he might). Eventually, "down" will seem awfully inviting and your down command will go smoothly.

Leash correction with almost any exercise except aggressive reactions is a simple snap of the leash. For example, you have put your dog on a sit-and-wait. He moves. Tell him "no" verbally. If he violates again, slide your left hand quickly to the leash's mid-point, snapping up with your left hand and down with the loop in your right hand. It's left up, right down – quickly. You may also move forward, stepping into the correction with your left foot, as this assists with control. Any time your dog violates his wait command, he must be led back to the initial spot he should not have left, reinforcing his wait. He is very much aware of his space and where everything is around him. He will learn.

Your non-verbal command for "down" is left hand at chest level, palm down, then motion downward. Your dog will ultimately see and obey this signal (and all others) on leash, off leash, and from 50 feet out as your training progresses.

## ***Lesson #7 – Return-to-Sit***

Simple enough. From a down, use your verbal "sit" along with your hand signal for sit.

These training exercises are to be combined as you and your dog progress from basic training. Work your dog as quickly as possible, both to keep his attention span and to reinforce that he needs to obey you quickly, not five minutes from now. If you begin to make these exercises a way of daily life, your results will be quicker and your dog's desire to work increases.

# ADDING THE POLISHING TOUCHES TO BASIC OBEDIENCE

***Review your training literature.*** With your increased knowledge and experience in training, you may find that reviewing this information is like reading it for the first time. Now, you can really relate to what it says. It will help you see *why* you're doing things this way.

***Brush up on each command,*** utilizing hand signal only, and a long leash (20-30 feet). Remember that hand signals increase your dog's attentiveness. He can no longer rely upon his own audio system; he has to *watch* you as well.

***Keep up your consistency – the real key to perfect dogs.*** The rewards are immediate *and* long-term.

***Vary the sequence of your commands.*** If you find that your dog is predicting the next command and performing it without you telling him to, then this is the polish you need. For example, place your dog on a "sit/wait", then "come". Next time, repeat the process. The *next* time, it's "sit/wait", then "down." Keep your canine on his toes. This also reinforces attentiveness.

***Vary your praise according to performance.*** If your dog requires a correction to follow through with a down command, for example, his praise is simply "good down." If he requires no correction, but obeys promptly, his praise should be both verbal and physical. After all, why try to excel if the praise is the same no matter what the effort?

***Watch your timing.*** Let's start looking for a more immediate response. He knows the command now; a quicker correction after the command is given gives him less time to play around. Ample time is counting "one thousand one." One thousand two, and you're too late.

***Add distractions.*** The type of environmental conditions you want your dog to perform in are the same conditions you should work in. When adding distractions, there are two things you will want to keep in mind:

a) Work on a gradient – desensitize your dog to distractions gradually. If you seem to lose his attention when working around other dogs, then you might begin working at a distance from other dogs. Slowly decrease the distance, thereby working closer to the distraction. After achieving control here, increase distractions by working around more than one dog.

b) In a distracting environment, you need to become firm and establish that *you* are the main attraction. You may find yourself having to give firmer correction than normal to achieve your dog's attentiveness.

***Make it all practical.*** Use your basic obedience. If you're still holding your dog back from lunging out of the door when you open it, why did you bother teaching him to sit and wait?

Having detailed actual physical training exercises, we are now ready to discuss the area of behavior modification; in a word – **problems!** This is the area of "behavior modification."

**Behavior Modification** consists of teaching your dog not to do the following:

1) Destructive chewing;
2) Jumping on people and furniture;
3) Robbing the trash can;
4) Mouthing (placing his teeth on you, which will intensify if allowed);
5) Digging holes;
6) Excessive barking;
7) Relieving himself in the house.

***Destructive chewing*** is the behavior problem probably most responsible for a dog leaving his original home and being adopted by an unsuspecting family, only to be moved again for the same reason. Although misunderstood, chewing is a very natural behavior. The solution is to direct the dog to his own toy (real bone) as discussed and not your furniture, carpet, and children's toys. This area was discussed in previous chapters regarding den areas. We will need to address the causes of this behavior, which are as follows: ***boredom, separation anxiety, chewing by association,*** and ***teething.***

In addressing boredom, the amount of time given to your dog is not the issue. It becomes very important how the time is spent. Your obedience training regimen helps greatly here. As I have pointed out previously, it is unrealistic and unfair to expect your canine to lie around and do nothing for the duration of his life. Likewise, it is unfair for him to be able to do exactly as he pleases, for he will be bored *and* restless without direction and guidance from you.

In a case of separation anxiety, the problem is predominantly due to a lack of confidence – a dog who is not confident to be left alone. This is not a genetic problem, but fueled by our desperate need to inflict our human emotions on our dogs. We discussed this at length previously with regard to overcoddling and babying canines. This is the result.

Chewing by association is a problem created by our reasoning. Again, refer to my sermon on allowing canines to have stuffed toys, socks, etc. Shortly after becoming familiar with the object's biting sensation, your dog directs his attention to the carpet, furniture, etc., and finds the sensations to be quite similar. Don't create this problem for yourself and your dog.

Teething takes a little time to get beyond. Provide acceptable chew toys for canine baby teeth and let him gnaw away.

## *Proofing Destructive Chewing*

Correcting this behavior while in progress is by far the best way to solve the problem. However, most behavior problems often take place when the owner is not in view. In order to rectify these problems, scenarios are highly recommended. With the use of scenarios, we can effectively solve unwanted behavior in ways which will avoid the dog directly associating the correction with us; rather, he learns that his own behavior caused unfortunate consequences.

Utilize a short spray of a cheap (preferably old) perfume. You received this as a Christmas gift three years ago. You detest it and have never worn it, but you can't bring yourself to get rid of it due to the possibility that Aunt Ethel could always make a trip through your bedroom sometime and ask you where it is and do you still enjoy it. Cheap fragrances contain a lot of alcohol which, over time, smells pretty gross. Trust me, your canine won't like it much at all. Proof furniture legs, toys, or whatever he's bothering with this fragrance.

Place your dog on a long sit-and-wait with objects he enjoys bothering on and around him. Do not allow him to move, sniff any of the objects, or place his mouth on one. Be creative! Have fun! Place an object on each paw and do not allow him to go for it. Rather than being cruel, it will help solve your chewing problem. After your set time, remove each item slowly, one by one, so he won't think it's all over. As you utilize this method, he will begin to associate those long sit-and-waits with those objects and begin to lose interest.

Always have available his dog bone – his acceptable chew toy. He will much prefer it because it satisfies the biting sensation for those growing (or grown) canine teeth like nothing else in the world can do.

If you have an existing destructive chewing problem, utilize your kennel while you are not at home. Don't allow him free roam of your house. He'll make the wrong choice every time until you train him differently. Don't give him opportunities to mess up while you're not there to correct the behavior. This is frustrating and expensive for you, and unfair to him.

## *Proofing Jumping on People and Furniture*

This problem is more easily solved. Your canine cannot differentiate between being carried around, being allowed to sleep on your beds and furniture, and jumping on people. Review the den area information and follow it. Don't carry your dog. Make it firm that he is not to jump on you or anyone else. When he tries, lift your leg so that it makes contact with his chest. Don't kick or push the dog with your leg; simply lift it so that he will run into this resistance on his own when he jumps. This plays with his equilibrium, and canines are very uncomfortable with that particular sensation.

Another proofing method is to utilize mice traps on furniture and beds. (This method is also very effective in proofing Fido's penchant for vacuuming the kitchen floor under the counters for dropped food.) Arm the traps with a small piece of lunch meat or cheese and let him have at it. He will not associate the correction with you, but with what he has done. This is one method of choice for cat fanciers in proofing kitties from kitchen counters, so have no fear about hurting your canine. If you want the problem to stop, you need to take affirmative action.

## *Proofing Robbing the Trash Can*

Preferred methods for a garbage-monger are either to arm with mice traps or to create a precarious pyramid of objects on top of your dog's object of desire, such as the kitchen trash can. When his wandering nose knocks pots, pans, cookie sheets, and what-have-you into a huge, ear-splitting (to him) crash on the floor, he has learned that the trash can is not as desirable as he once believed.

## *Mouthing*

This subject was discussed in previous chapters in conjunction with levels of aggression. We discussed scruffing as proper correction and dominance rolls to keep the problem from growing. There is no way to "proof," per se, for mouthing.

Your dominance and leadership are everything here. This can be a dangerous behavior problem which must be dealt with immediately.

## *Digging*

This problem should already be solved by following the previous information regarding providing a den area for your dog inside your home. Later, as he is trained and proofed from problem behavior, his den will be your home, without a kennel, as he learns to be trusted alone. Also, do not leave your dog on a tie-down, unattended, outside. Left alone, a canine's natural instinct is to *dig a den* for survival purposes, as discussed in previous chapters. This is a behavior problem that need not be allowed to start. You control it.

## *Excessive Barking*

Interestingly enough, what some people view as the problem of excessive barking is often viewed by others as desirable behavior in their dogs. For the purposes of analyzing this behavior, we can break it down into three aspects. One is when the puppy or dog barks when left alone. The second is when the dog barks when the owner is at home, and the third is the problem of barking in regard to aggressive behavior in older dogs. Barking or whining is one of the few ways a canine has of expressing himself.

Solving the problem of barking when the owner is home is much more easily accomplished than when he isn't at home. Before undertaking a course of correction, we must determine the cause behind excessive barking. The most common reasons for excessive barking (keeping in mind that the dog is generally either barking at something or for something) are:

1) To protest isolation;
2) To gain a response from another person, animal, or object; and
3) As an alarm toward unidentified sounds, movements, or objects.

What is viewed as the problem is often a symptom of the problem. The excessive barker is responding to stress in a situation in which he vents through barking, whining, or howling.

When you realize that the dog is barking for attention, and the owner pops in to punish the dog after he has been barking up a storm, what has occurred, in essence, is that the barking is being reinforced by the owner. In other words, he is teaching his dog that barking is what gets him the attention that all dogs crave and desire.

To correct the problem of excessive barking due to isolation, the solution should be obvious. Stop isolating the dog! Also, stop reinforcing the barking. When he is about to start barking is the time to use an intervening stimulus to distract him from the bark which is about to occur.

One of the simplest ways to distract a dog from barking is the use of a "throw can." This is an empty can with a few marbles, pennies, or pebbles in it that can be thrown to the ground in his general direction with the word, "No!" Dropping a metal plate or pan, or a heavy rap on a window away from the *source* of the dog's barking can be equally as effective.

Barking can also be viewed sometimes as attention-seeking behavior, often a byproduct of separation anxiety, the causes of which were discussed previously. (Refer to Chapter 3, "My Dog is My Baby.") The best approach to solve this type of excessive barking is to: (1) Stop babying the dog; and (2) Build his confidence by teaching independence via leadership values. In due time, he will learn to trust your judgment and ultimately feel secure.

Dogs with protective energy fall into the second category of "alarm barking." This is barking at an unidentified sound or movement which is perceived as a non-threatening one. Owners who desire a bold "watch dog" type often make the error of encouraging this type of barking by reinforcing it with excited comments such as "What is that?" as the dog is barking with no encouragement whatsoever.

As soon as the dog barks a few times, the owner should command the dog to a different part of the house. (When obedience training on leash, make sure leash is in hand to enforce the command, so owner doesn't chase dog.) In this way, the dog is taught to sound the alarm, then seek the owner. This will be a desirable trait in your dog as he matures. When a puppy responds to this, the owner is to quietly praise him, then remain quiet. If the dog turns again toward the source of the barking, he should be commanded to come to his owner until he settles down. ***Do not scold, discipline loudly, or hold your dog's mouth shut!*** This will heighten anxiety and contribute to the barking. As always, physical punishment should be avoided as well.

When the problem of barking when left alone is being addressed, it should be understood that the problem should first be under control when the owners are at home with the dog. When accomplished at home with the dog, similar scenarios may be arranged when it appears to your dog that you are *not* at home. Act as though you are leaving. Close the drapes, jiggle the car keys, put on your jacket, close the door, and start your car. Sneak back (not too near the doorway or your dog will smell your presence). Introduce distractions which your dog associates with a feeling of well-being related to quiet times in the daily routine. These can include the rattling of a dinner dish or doorknob, or turning on the radio or television. (Obviously, any distraction that has stimulated barking in the past should not be used.) For owners who must be away for long periods of time daily, such as eight to 12 hours, leaving a television or radio on low volume has proven helpful.

Concentration on the down-wait in obedience training gradually (to the point where you can be out of view for 15 minutes) is also helpful. Puppies have been corrected with these methods in as little as one day or as much as six weeks.

Most puppies between 12 and 26 weeks of age will begin announcing their presence to strangers or attracting the attention of their owners by barking and sounding territorial alarms at other animals. The secret of preventing the natural characteristics from developing into a behavior problem is by avoiding reinforcement of the behavior. Simply put - ignore the barking! (Please be aware that shouting at the puppy to shut up tends to reinforce his barking.)

If sound or movement causes excessive barking, the dog should be taken to the area from which the sound originated and allowed to investigate while the owner reassures him that there is nothing to fear.

In the instance of excessive barking related to aggressive behavior in the mature dog, the home environment itself is usually what teaches excessive barking. Examples of this are owners who are nervous about their own safety or owners who isolate their dogs. Barrier frustration also contributes in this scenario, such as viewing fences and windows while isolated.

The barking dog tends to be a "worry wart" and usually a dominant type in relation to its owner. Therefore, the overall effect of obedience training in terms of establishing the proper role of leadership with the dog is a definite must. To leave this type of behavior problem unattended can lead to the aggressive dog moving further toward biting people.

Finally, I have seen poor results when owners have used tranquilizers or anti-bark shock collars. The barking tends to recur when the medication or collar is no longer utilized. Aside from the cruelty factor in these methods, there really is no substitute for quality time spent teaching your dog.

## *Housebreaking*

Although the issue of housebreaking is probably one of the most frustrating problems with dogs, it is also one of the easiest to solve. This topic is discussed in detail in Chapter 3, "Wrong Thing Number 3 – "I Always Leave Food and Water Out." However, there are a few points I will cover at this juncture.

Most puppies and dogs can be housebroken in a very short time. They may also be conditioned to relieve themselves in one area, on command. The quickest method of housebreaking is a five-step process consisting of the following:

1) Correction and Praise
2) Consistency
3) Confinement
4) Schedules
5) Proper Nutrition

## *Correction and Praise*

The first thing to remember is that your dog cannot reason as you do. Therefore, you must also understand that you can correct, but not punish (associated with emotional guilt). Timing is everything. In order to solve the problem, the dog must be corrected while the bad behavior is in progress. The praise must be applied while the good behavior is in progress. Don't wait until the dog gets to the door to praise. The proper conditioning is to take him to the designated area of your yard to relieve himself and praise him while he is in the act. Act as though you've just inherited a million bucks from Aunt Bertha! Remember your praising tone.

## *Consistency*

Typically, most puppies under 14 weeks of age will need to relieve themselves every two to four hours. Of course, they also need to go potty after they play, sleep, or eat. If the effort to get puppy out to potty is consistent, puppy will be as well.

## *Confinement*

The crate is the method of choice to use for your housebreaking effort. It will be used when no one has the time or patience to watch the pup. Dogs instinctively will not soil the areas in which they sleep and eat. Because of the physical limitations of the infant puppy, however, you can see that it would not be feasible for a family that spends a lot of time away to start with a puppy. Instead, the older dog may be more suitable.

## *Schedules*

By putting your dog on a strict food and water-monitoring schedule, you will have a good opportunity to condition his internal clock. Most puppies will need to eat and drink more because they are still in the process of growing. Even at this level, careful monitoring is needed.

## *Housebreaking an Older Dog*

When you set out to housebreak an older dog, the principles involved are the same as with a puppy, but the application may vary. Like any habit, the more ingrained it becomes or the longer it persists, the more difficult it is to break. However, it is not an insurmountable problem.

When dogs have persisted for months or years in relieving themselves in the house, it points to an overall lack of rapport between the dog and his owner(s) or, at the very least, to the dog having what you might call an improper self-concept. Therefore, the situation first needs to be rectified through owner education because it is rarely, if ever, the dog's fault. Unless we are successful in instituting a change in the way owners interact with their dogs, we cannot be successful in changing the way in which a dog reacts, both to them and to his environment.

As discussed earlier, dogs inherently are pack animals. Every pack has its leader (or alpha dog). The canine-human relationship works best when dogs perceive their owners as the pack leader. Dogs are content to follow. They are happiest with the owner who puts things in black and white, one who is consistent, one who requires something from them, and yet one who doesn't make unrealistic demands upon them.

Obedience training is the best way to establish the proper role of leadership with a dog (partly by eliciting a following response). The learning process also has a cumulative effect on a dog, which is to say that the more you teach a dog, the easier it is for him to learn, and the easier it is for you to teach him new things. This, of course, carries over to housebreaking or to anything else you are trying to teach a dog.

First, you must be certain that the problem is not a physiological one. This can be ascertained by a thorough veterinary exam, including fecal tests.

Second, it should be noted that sometimes, problems of micturition (marking territory) and submissive urination (and the rarity of submissive or nervous defecation) should not be confused with a housebreaking problem. A housebreaking approach to these issues will usually compound rather than alleviate them.

The control-confinement method of housebreaking as discussed in Chapter 3 plays a vital role. While reinforcing a canine's natural desire for a clean den, it also limits his opportunity to make mistakes, thereby hugely reducing the over-and-over habit of going potty in the house, and reinforcing the right habit of doing business

41

outside in one spot. Obviously, a dog with housebreaking issues should never be allowed free roam of the house, unmonitored visually and/or without his control mechanism, or leash.

I am a firm believer in the principle of behavior modification, which may be defined as a combination of firmness and consistency in correction in conjunction with praise at the proper time. These should be combined with the aforementioned control-confinement situations.

This can easily be shown by using a common analogy to define "conditioned response." The key words in this definition are **firmness, consistency,** and **timing.** For example, you see a steak on the table and you haven't eaten in days. However, every time you approach the table, you experience a significant electrical shock, one that knocks you to the floor. How long would it take you to decide it's not worth trying to get the steak? Answers usually range from one time to a few times. My point is that it is a relatively short time before the decision is reached.

Here are the subtleties behind the "why." First, the shock (correction) occurred before you were able to get the steak. Timing is the essence of training because canines do not have the abilities of logic and reasoning like humans. Happily, because of the lack of this roadblock, they may be conditioned even more quickly. You cannot teach a dog that he "can't" when he already "has." Second, the correction was consistent; it happened every time you approached the steak. If not, you would obviously continue in your effort. Third, the correction was firm. If it was not, it would not have deterred you from your course of action – the motivation to eat. Your dog can also reach this conclusion on where to relieve himself almost as quickly. The bottom line is that once you have been conditioned and trained in the steak situation, you give up trying. At that point, how do you know the electricity has been shut off? Once dogs are effectively housebroken, it is rare to see regression. They are (say it with me) "creatures of habit!"

I suggest correcting the older dog by either a long leash to the collar or the use of a "throw can." (Leash correction has been covered previously, as has the thrown can method for excessive barking.) Remember, however, that as important as the adverse conditioning is to breaking a bad habit, the positive reinforcement of praise and petting for a job well done is equally important. If, after you were shocked at the table, you were taken out, given a meal, some money, and a pat on the back, you would certainly prefer to eat out rather than to sit home, continually being unsuccessful in getting the steak and getting hungrier all the time.

Sometimes, a chart kept on urination and defecation habits can be helpful. Reviewing the chart will assist you in seeing what your dog's daily routine is.

Unfortunately, space does not permit all the specifics and/or contingency approaches because there are a lot of variables involved. This is when the individuality of the dog sometimes makes it difficult to give blanket advice.

In summary, it's up to the dog owner to be consistent enough in applying the proper consequence to the dog's behavior – to make it a simple choice for the dog of where to do his stuff. The less success your dog has in urinating and defecating in the house, the sooner he will give up trying.

# CHAPTER 5:
## SOME HORROR STORIES

I knew that by the time you got to this chapter, you would be very used to the word "consistency." The following will help you to see why this issue matters so much. I am going to share with you some of the results of inconsistency in training, violation of methods, and complete deviation from both.

The first real-life scenario involves a dog who shall remain nameless. This dog was not worked (trained) on a daily basis. A canine who lies around day after day with no job description becomes bored and eventually reverts more to canine instinct since there is no leadership in the pack. She also had a cushion in her kennel, a no-no as discussed in conjunction with destructive chewing. The first problem was chewing up the cushion - dangerous for her physically, expensive, and a mess for her owners. However, once she had had a chance to gnaw on a cushion, her appetite for fabric increased, not because she loved cushions, but because she needed a bone to chew on, not a pillow. To her, the biting sensation was the same. Her chewing progressed from the kennel cushion to the family room carpeting, then to the sofa. (By this time, you should have asked yourself why she was wandering loose in the house with no eyes-on monitoring.) Because the small children in the pack were not made to stay out of her space, especially the vital den area, the daughter teased and provoked the dog one too many times and received a serious bite to the face, requiring not only stitches, but reconstructive surgery. Now, if she ever had hopes of being a model or an actress, she will have to ask her parents why they didn't stop her before this happened.

Was our nameless canine a bad dog? She was treated as one. She was removed from the home, which, by the time a bite occurs to a family member, is the best solution in the absence of professional help and a big change of interaction with the dog. My point is that she was not a bad dog; her behavior resulted from poor conditioning – human reasoning and deviation from the process. She could have been a wonderful asset to her family - loyal and protective. Instead, she paid the ultimate price.

In situation number two, our nameless canine was babied endlessly for years – carried, coddled, cooed to. Slept in the family's beds and sofas. Called her own shots. Demanded her owners' affection and achieved it. Along came human infant. Although aware of the ramifications, the rules went by the wayside. So did the dog, permanently, when she tagged the infant while she slept on the sofa. This is irresponsibility which rebounded on two innocents, baby and dog, not to mention the owners' anguish at having to give up the dog after seven years.

You will recall the previous chapters in which I discussed isolation and aggression. I have encountered families who leave their dogs unattended in a fenced yard, either running or on a tie-down. In these instances, I have arrived on the scene of a nuisance barker (due to isolation) who was permanently silenced by an irate neighbor who tossed a piece of bologna laced with antifreeze over the fence, or was picked off by a shotgun while the owner was away. Please do not place your dog in an indefensible situation such as this, not to mention that a dog left to its own devices can be a hyperactive maniac when brought into the house.

I have also had the sad experience of seeing dogs euthanized due to being fed a human diet. Besides the various health consequences for the dog, a prolonged toothache from poor nutrition can eventually produce an "unprovoked" bite, meaning that a dog who has been placid forever suddenly lashes out when touched, simply from pain. The owners don't understand that it's from tooth decay and poor diet; they simply believe that the dog suddenly "snapped" one day. This is not the case. There is always a reason. Most dogs display behavior problems due to conditioning (what is allowed and how the dog is handled in the home) rather than temperament. Stick to your veterinarian's choice of dog food for your canine and leave cheeseburgers out of the plan.

In summary, none of these events had to occur. I believe that dog owners who have experienced these problems without training, just owning, simply did not know. The ones who were made aware paid unnecessary, very costly prices by doing things through human reasoning. Please, put your new knowledge of canine behavior to use. The same way that an individual who desires to learn one of the martial arts does not tell the instructor that he is wrong and proceed to go about the art form his own way, a person desiring to learn about canine behavior, interaction, and training, follows the rules. No one pays for a college course and informs his professor that he would rather complete the course his own way, or refuses to complete an assignment because he doesn't think it's important. Canine interaction and training is the same way. All have consequences.

Now, let's go on to some positive stories of dogs whose owners have followed the process, with some remarkable results to show for it.

# CHAPTER 6:
# SUCCESS STORIES

Diligent training and adherence to what you have been taught truly does pay off! Many students have successfully brought their canines through this process with flying colors. They are a pleasure to watch on the field and in daily living. Their control levels are outstanding. Through understanding canine behavior and application of knowledge, their dogs are truly valued family members who have privileges many "pets" don't have. These dogs showcase their intelligence and obedience in awesome ways.

One particular family put in the effort to have their multiple dogs actually working on long lines on the third training session. Obedience was nearly flawless. Behavior modification issues, such as housebreaking and canine pack rivalry aggression, disappeared. These dogs (and they are no exception to yours) got so into training (a work ethic with the motivation of positive reinforcement from their owners) that they lived for it. These people made it a way of life, as it will be for the duration of their dogs' lives.

Another family had a problem with canine aggression toward not only strangers, but outside family members, knocking at the door. Aside from that issue, this particular dog also had a very timid, shy personality. He would urinate submissively at the slightest provocation. His personality was from *temperament*, but *conditioning* turned it around. He is what is termed a "fear aggressor," which I touch upon briefly later. At first afraid of the leash, he gained more and more confidence as we worked. On the last occasion that I worked with this canine, he was beyond eager to work on a leash. The submissive urination has stopped. The growling has stopped. His confidence is way up. He is valued, he is appreciated, and he works hard for it. He has a purpose to exist and strong leadership to guide him throughout his life. This is the ultimate goal of training. There are many other possibilities open for this dog now. He can undergo agility training, flyball…whatever his owners may desire to pursue. Remember, canines do have a working mentality!

Yet another student has achieved amazing results with her dog. Living alone, she wanted not only protection out of her canine, but also control over his guarding. A guard dog without training is a very dangerous canine. Diligent adherence to what she was taught brought results that have other female students desiring to achieve the same thing with their own dogs. Not only that, but this woman has also gained much self-confidence of her own. There is a misconception that men are better trainers than women, but knowledge and hard work prove that to be untrue. You can achieve whatever you desire with your canine. I have video footage to prove it! It is absolutely possible for a four foot, eleven inch female to have ultimate control of and leadership over her German Shepherd or Rottweiler. It's all in what you learn about canine behavior and how you apply it.

Finally, there is the story of the mixed breed Shepherd, destined for nothing, waiting for nothing in an animal shelter to come to the aid of the very best of my students. This woman had been brutally physically assaulted and traumatized. Another single lady, she was understandably fearful of living by herself after this event. The dog she chose could be your own. She had no idea of the capabilities of this mixed breed dog until she learned about canine behavior and the application of training, tapping into his intelligence and what he was all about. For years, I have used these two as an example to my other students when I teach in the field. Obedience on command is flawless every time. This dog is not only an ace at obedience, but has also earned himself a Good Citizenship award and is used as a service dog, helping in hospitals and other institutions where his services are needed.

These two are a remarkable example of not only what can be done to solve problems with *your* dog, but of realizing his true potential. Properly conditioned and patiently trained, your dog will amaze you.

# CHAPTER 7:
## HAVE YOU LEARNED ANYTHING?

After all is said and done, it's too apparent to realize that canines are far underrated by treating them as "pets." Training is not for everyone, for there are some who simply want fuzzy and cuddly. This attitude is unfair to both owner and dog for the simple reason that "fuzzy" and "cuddly" always equal problems. These problems then become a dog's "fault" for not "understanding" what you expect. Human reasoning and canines do *not* mix. Your dog is not a baby; he is one hundred percent Canis lupus familiaris. From three pounds to 160 pounds, their nature is the same. It is only fair and humane to learn to understand the nature of a creature one claims to love. If you love your dog, you will train him.

# CHAPTER 8:
# BITS AND PIECES

This final chapter will address various issues with regard to canines. For the sake of simplicity, I have simply called it "Bits and Pieces."

## *PICKING YOUR PUPPY*

Selecting a puppy can be a very long and drawn-out process. Here are some things to consider in making your selection:

1) Do you have sufficient room for the breed of dog you desire? He will need space to grow.

2) You will need to investigate the dog's family history. In many cases, aggression toward people and other dogs can be an inherited trait. Improper breeding could also be a contributing factor to such behavior.

3) Learning the characteristics of the breed you desire is always helpful. Breeds have different characteristics and purposes. The Husky is bred for pulling, the beagle is a natural hunter, the collie is a natural herding canine, the bloodhound a natural tracker, etc. What people consider to be behavior problems in some dogs is many times an integral part of the dog's natural instincts.

4) Selecting the proper temperament is probably the most important consideration in a search for the right puppy. Many professionals perform a temperament test. By taking the puppy and having him submit (roll over on his back to expose his vital organs), we can get an idea about how receptive

he will be to training. However, it does depend upon the owner's purpose. If it is a family dog that you have in mind, you may want the most submissive dog. On the other hand, the working dog community (police departments, ring sport members, etc.) prefer a more aggressive and energetic canine.

5) Adopting an older dog has many advantages. In most cases, the dog is already housebroken and, hopefully, any other behavior problems are already taken care of. The only disadvantage is your inability to know the true background of this dog. In such a case, you should interact with the dog as much as possible before you make a final decision. As always, it is important to receive some sort of professional training to ensure that you have a well-behaved family member.

Take your time during the selection process. After all, this dog is going to be a family member for the next 10 to15 years.

## <u>TIPS FOR KENNEL TRAINING</u>

All dogs, whether domesticated or wild, have a natural desire to create a den area. In the wild, a dog will always create a den for himself. The den may be in the form of a hole in the ground, a cave, or the cavity of a tree. He will live there most of his life for shelter, socializing, and procreation of the species. In addition to den areas, there are territorial boundaries which are guarded daily and violently, if necessary.

The first thing to address when the new dog arrives is the introduction of a new den area. I recommend a wire crate. It needs to be placed in the family's living area, where much family time is spent. This allows the dog to view his entire territory, which makes it less stressful for him than being locked in a garage or separate room, or even worse, isolated outside. Using a crate will also help the housebreaking process because dogs do not like to soil the area where they sleep and eat.

A puppy may not like his new home at first. Many howl or whine through the night, causing mass confusion for the new owners. The typical reaction would be to offer human comfort. For the first few days, the young one has to get used to his new territory and the fact that this is a new pack, without Mom to pave the way. Ignoring the puppy's frantic pleas for attention is frustrating and can cause sleepless nights for awhile, but given time and patience, you will get past this issue. Please be aware that I am not instructing that the puppy should spend all day every day in the kennel, but kennel time during the day *while you are at home* really helps alleviate stress, yet helps the puppy establish the kennel as his den area. Kennel time at night is a must.

After a few days, the kennel becomes a very safe and warm den area. When used properly, a kennel can be a wonderful training tool, although I do not recommend it for the lifetime of a dog.

1) Place the kennel in an area where your family spends most of its time.

2) Leave the lights, TV, and/or radio on for that lived-in feeling.

3) Feed and water in the kennel for housebreaking purposes.

4) Never leave equipment (leash and collar) or other foreign objects in the kennel (especially blankets and stuffed animals, etc.)

5) Place acceptable chew toys in the kennel.

6) When addressing behavior problems, confine the puppy unless you have the time and patience to address him. Also, he must be monitored 100% of the time when he is out of the kennel, as behavior problems are started in just this way. Utilize leash and collar while puppy is out of the kennel for control mechanism.

7) Never use the kennel as a form of punishment. This will set your training process back.

The Cost of a Crate
Crates can cost from $50 upward, depending upon the size and type of crate and the source.

The Cost of Not Buying a Crate
Your shoes, books, table legs, chairs, sofas, carpet, rugs, electrical, telephone, and computer wire, emergency veterinarian bills, your sanity

** The benefit of a crate is your dog's safety and your peace of mind.

## THE KNUCKLEHEAD SYNDROME

All the time you spent monitoring your dog has made your dream a reality. Your puppy is finally housebroken! That is, you *thought* he was. Where did that spot on the carpet come from? You thought he was done teething. What happened to your shoe? Didn't he already learn how to "sit" and "wait"? So, where does he think *he's* going?

Welcome to canine adolescence, which can emerge anywhere from six to 18 months of age. He has lost all of that soft puppy fur and is almost his full height. He may look like an adult, but don't let that fool you. Like human teenagers, dogs can be gangly and awkward at this stage. They have adult teeth, but still have the physical need to chew in order to properly set their teeth in the jawbone.

The adolescent canine has more energy than he (or you, for that matter) knows what to do with. If you are into physical activities such as jogging or walking, this is the perfect time to include him in those activities. If you are more sedentary, maybe this is a good time to change that. If nothing else, a good game of fetch the Frisbee or ball can go a long way toward alleviating excess energy in your adolescent dog.

Now is not the time to leave your dog unsupervised in your home. A crate is still a vital piece of equipment for you and your dog. Chewing, slips in housebreaking, and general destruction of property are still possibilities at this stage. It is better to prevent these behaviors than to try to reverse them.

Romance is in the air at around eight to 12 months of age. Males will mark territory (lifting legs, kicking up dirt) and females will have their first heat. The best thing to do is to spay or neuter early – normally, before seven months of age. Besides helping to avoid problems with indoor urination, you can reduce same-sex aggression, loss of attention span due to hormones, accidental matings, and a host of other problems attributable to the "call of the wild."

A canine teenager, even if neutered or spayed, will sometimes have trouble with attention span. There will be times when it will seem as if he has had no training at all. Handle this by going back to the basics of training.

Re-teach any commands that your dog has seemingly forgotten, and remember to use positive reinforcement to reward him when he does well.

To help you and your dog survive the adolescent phase:

1) Provide plenty of exercise and training;
2) Continue to use the crate when you cannot monitor;
3) Spay or neuter;
4) Keep training sessions short and fun;
5) Be patient. It won't last forever!

## *THE AGGRESSOR*

Physical Causes
The Fear Aggressor
Dominance and Leadership
The Professional Aggressor
Games
Breeding

Experts have their theories regarding canine aggression and the family dog. Let us begin to understand what aggression is and how it develops. Like any other behavior problem, it must be proofed. In other words, after training and behavior modification have been completed, there must be tests to see if the behavior has been eliminated. Unfortunately, there is no way to proof this behavior. We may also conclude that there is no guarantee that a dog with this problem will never bite. Because of a dog's nature, there is always the possibility that even the kindest canine family member can become an aggressor.

## *PHYSICAL CAUSES*

The first step in working with any behavior problem is identifying its origin, first ruling out the possibility of a physical cause. Some health-related issues which can result in aggressive behavior include tooth decay, rabies, or any health condition which is causing a dog physical pain. It is important to have regular check-ups with your veterinarian. Not only does this keep your dog current on his vaccinations, but a veterinarian can spot a potential health problem. In a case of aggression, your veterinarian is your first step.

## *THE FEAR AGGRESSOR*

One of the most common forms of correction used by an untrained dog owner is hitting a dog or resorting to some other type of physical abuse. Unknowingly, this handler uses human reactions to try to solve the problem. The dog, on the other hand, cannot understand the overall message being given. Therefore, he establishes a fear of forward body movements, particularly hands moving toward his face or body. He doesn't learn that his behavior is unacceptable; he is learning never to get caught.

If a dog is being physically abused, he begins to believe that he must be defensive for his own safety. The development of defensive instincts produces an animal who doesn't have a lot of confidence, and he may show some form of aggression. In this case, the owner has to have a firm understanding that the idea is to instill confidence, not fear. Hitting your dog is never the way to go.

## *DOMINANCE AND LEADERSHIP*

There should be many leadership boundaries within the home when raising a dog to be a family member. Many families inadvertently encourage dominant aggression. Often, even the simplest game of tug-of-war becomes fuel for the fire. The dog begins to understand that he is winning, enhancing his natural desire for promotion within his pack. Most owners are under the misconception that this is a healthy way to play with their dogs. It may be a very costly lesson to learn!

Another dominance issue is the den and the role it plays in the dominance hierarchy. Defending the den and territory are essential to a canine's survival. Many humans take this for granted and allow the dog to share their den areas (beds, sofas, etc.) This is a very dangerous practice, especially if small children are in the home.

Ironically, most of the dogs who suffer from this kind of disorder weigh 25 pounds or less. The problem is that most of the biting goes largely unnoticed and the media will never report it. The owners may even excuse or deny the behavior under the guise of "nipping." A "nip" is a first level bite, as you will recall.

## *ISOLATION VERSUS SOCIALIZATION*

Isolation can be described as a situation in which the dog is unable to socialize or view family and territory. Here are a few examples:

1. Locked in a garage;

2. Attached to a tree in the yard (he cannot go to shelter from cruelty or adverse weather);

3. Locked in a room (building frustration which can lead to additional behavior problems such as separation anxiety or hyperactivity upon release, which may or may not include submissive urination);

4. Locked in a basement (no stimulation for delicate hearing).

Clearly, proper socialization is needed, especially where a dominant and independent breed is concerned. In order to achieve a high social standard for the dog, he must be able to live within the social structure. Kennels and crates are often used as den areas within the home. Their use reduces anxiety and the preponderance for aggression which stems from it. Eventually, it becomes normal for the dog to see visitors as he views his territory and the things in it.

A dog on a chain is the most common of canine aggressors. This unfortunate dog is left outside to deal with the elements, teased by outsiders, and more than likely abused by his owners. This type of dog would probably be the most difficult to correct. It is hard to use a leash and collar on this dog because of his conditioned immunity to correction (constant tugging and pulling at his chain in order to be free). Changing this kind of dog requires a great handler with a lot of patience.

# THE PROFESSIONAL AGGRESSOR

Sport dogs, such as ring sport dogs, Schutzhund dogs, commercial guard dogs, and working dogs (police or military canines) are usually encouraged to display aggression on command as needed for their duties in the field. These animals are known to be free of fear and capable of being driven to epic aggressive proportions. Whenever dealing with this kind of canine, extreme caution is advised. In fact, unless you are a canine professional, *don't!*

Confrontations with the commercial guard dog can, and almost always are, lethal. This dog usually does not discriminate or differentiate his victims. Normally, no one is around to control his aggression in any event. That's the entire purpose – to protect property from theft and vandalism at odd hours when no humans are present to guard property. A confrontation with this dog is almost sure to be catastrophic.

The personal protection dog, if properly trained, should not display raw aggression like working dogs or commercial guard dogs. If an owner would like to condition his dog for this kind of work ethic, it is wise to research the kinds of training methods used. Any method other than one which utilizes repetition and praise should be avoided. Only disreputable trainers use pain and humiliation. Talk to others who have been through the process you are seeking. Seek professional canine training resources.

# PLAYING GAMES

People tend to encourage behavior that pleases them more than what is truly healthy for their dogs. The typical puppy learns at an early age how to roughhouse and mouth on his owner. However, it is the family which pays the biggest penalty because it becomes a learned behavior for the dog. By the time a puppy reaches the four-month-old stage, this behavior has become part of his personality.

It is not recommended to leave children and this type of dog unsupervised. Children like to run, and in many cases, the dog will view them as moving prey. The "tug-of-war" games, in most cases, are the methods of choice in professional aggression training.

# BREEDING

Different breeds of canines possess varying characteristics. This should be considered when purchasing or adopting a dog. There may be certain hereditary traits from previous generations in addition to the actual known breed characteristics. Temperament should be considered as well if the intent is to have a family member.

Now that we understand some of the causes for canine aggression, we may be able to find solutions to some of the problems associated with this behavior. It may also be wise to undertake a total overhaul of the way the family interacts with the family dog. You may be saving a life!

## *CAUTION!*

If aggression is directed toward immediate family members, removing the dog from the home is the best recommendation. Aggression cannot be guaranteed not to resurface as with any other behavior problem. With aggression on the rise, I hope that people who are suffering from this problem would seek the help of canine professionals. In addition, this is a problem which cannot be rectified by a textbook or obedience class. Denial results in the ultimate disaster.

## *CIVIL LIABILITY AND DOGS*

While laws and definitions vary from state to state, the intent of these laws remains constant: to civilly empower the victim of a dog bite. I could elaborate endlessly on this subject and quote various state laws, but my main point is not to cite statutes and case law, but to instruct owners of dogs as to civil liability and the precautions which can be taken to avoid a dog bite.

Therefore, if possible, fence in the yard or property. Place "No Trespassing" signs in visible areas, and have a picture of a dog with bared teeth for those who cannot read. Secure your gates or doors with padlocks and tell your neighbors what to do if your dog escapes. Leave them your work number or an emergency contact number so you can be notified immediately if necessary.

Most importantly, establishing and maintaining *control* of your dog through training eliminates this issue entirely.

## *THE OUTDOOR K-9*

What about the outdoor dog on a chain, in the dog run, or in the garage? Most responses are very dogmatic:

"I want him outside, that's why!"

"He prefers to be outside."

"A dog is supposed to be outside."

"He messes in the house."

"He chews and jumps when he's in the house."

"Too much hair, and he smells like a dog."

"He doesn't leave my visitors alone when they're here."

"Shouldn't he have fresh air and exercise?"


There are often other reasons that a dog remains outside, such as allergies or elderly/handicapped members being present at the residence. We know that we would make as many excuses to keep the dog as there are adversities to doing so.

The hair issue is a reality for the dog, but this problem can be greatly reduced with proper grooming and care.

Every now and then, even the most housebroken dog may have an accident, which could be due to physiological reasons.

Finally, not every dog desires fresh air and exercise 24 hours a day. If the dog is outside, provide him with a lot of yard and a good dog house. The dog house should be painted light colors in the summertime to reduce heat absorption, and darker colors for winter to make the den warmer. Make sure the house is well-insulated. Cedar chips will help in that regard. The outdoor dog will need additional fat in his diet in the winter and less in the summer.

However, most outside dogs are there for several reasons, the first being the fact that the owners simply want it that way and don't think it 's important enough to change the dog's lifestyle. Secondly, they may have tried to make the transition, but were unsuccessful. If the second reason applies, this book will help to address these issues. If you insist on having the dog outside, without having an open mind, there is no point in my trying to change that. But, then, I ask you – what's the point of owning a dog? Then again, if you desire an outdoor pet, consider horses, cows, pigs, etc.

There are many animals that can and do survive in harsh elements, and maybe the dog is not your thing. However, if you've read this far, that's probably not you!

# <u>*SUBMISSIVE URINATION*</u>

Submissive urination is very different from a housebreaking issue due to the fact that it is completely involuntary. This usually happens when a puppy or dog is being subordinate to a higher-ranking pack member. It is a normal act of submission, although hardly acceptable in the home. This behavior will eventually pass. However, here are some ideas and techniques to help make the transition a little quicker.

First of all, you can't *correct* the dog for this behavior as it will only enhance the problem. Also keep in mind that we, as humans, can be intimidating in both size and tone to a dog, especially where a puppy is concerned. Kneeling down helps because it is a less threatening posture. Praise under the chin or on the chest. Many puppies and dogs may find that petting on the head is an intrusive gesture, not to mention that it obstructs vision.

In addition, be aware of unrealistic practices that encourage this behavior, such as emotional homecomings and departures, visitors or family that may overstimulate puppy, and unwanted activity of children with regard to the dog. These episodes are not at all reasons to isolate the dog, but makes the need to educate the people around you more urgent. Make any greeting low-key to build more confidence and independence. Training and proper socialization will help with this issue. Also, leaving the water bowl down with free access doesn't help the problem.

# GLOSSARY OF TERMS

*** DOG ***

A flesh-eating mammal.

**Aggression:** Unprovoked attack; practice of making unprovoked attacks; marked by driving energy or hostile, injurious or destructive behavior, especially when caused by frustration.

\*\* *All dogs are capable of aggression. Any and all forms should always be taken very seriously.* \*\*

**Attitude:** Mental position or feeling with regard to a fact or state.

\*\* *You must maintain a positive, confident attitude with your dog. If you doubt yourself, your dog will, too.* \*\*

**Command:** A direct order to achieve a specific goal or objective.

\*\* *You must learn to command, not request, your dog.* \*\*

**Conditioning:** To put in proper condition for action or use. To adapt, modify, or mold to respond in a particular way.

\*\* *Properly conditioning your dog will result in a lifestyle both comfortable and pleasant for the entire family.* \*\*

**Correct:** To make right.

|  | |
|---|---|
| ** | *You cannot punish your dog.  You can correct unacceptable behavior.*　** |
| **Dominate:** | To prevail over all others, exhibit authority and/or control. |
| ** | *In a dog's mind, it is very important that you, the dog owner, dominate your pack.  If you do not, he will surely try to dominate for you.*　** |
| **Guard Dog:** | A dog who makes a living by simply biting at his own discretion, with no remorse. |
| ** | *Guard dogs are for commercial use only, never intended for a family atmosphere.*　** |
| **Leadership:** | The ability to guide or direct. |
| ** | *It is vital that you establish and maintain leadership of your dog.*　** |
| **Method:** | A procedure or process for achieving an end or objective. |
| ** | *The method that I have shared with you is one of positive reinforcement.  When applied properly, it is the most effective way to teach your dog, and is ultimately love channeled in a positive way.*　** |
| **Monitor:** | Watch, check, or observe for a specific purpose. |
| ** | *You will need to monitor your dog during the teaching phase of training.  Without monitoring, no one can be sure of proper behavior.*　** |
| **Pack:** | A group of dogs. |
| ** | *Any time you bring a dog into your home, you create a pack, which will consist of you, your family, and any other dogs within the home.*　** |
| **Pecking Order:** | The basic pattern of social organization; social hierarchy. |
| ** | *In every pack, there is an "alpha," or lead dog.  Make sure that is you!*　** |

**Personal
Protection Dog:** A well-rounded, sociable family dog who has simply been taught how to bite, when to bite, and when not to bite for the personal use of a family. This dog is one whose teaching has been geared toward "real life" application.

\*\* *This is the most effective and reliable type of dog to use for a person or family.* \*\*

**Philosophy:** A critical study of fundamental beliefs and the grounds for them.

\*\* *It is my belief that training you is just as important as training your dog.* \*\*

**Prey:** An animal taken for food by another.

\*\* *Often, balls, adults, children, other dogs, and other animals are viewed as prey.* \*\*

**Prey Drive:** The desire to hunt or chase.

\*\* *All dogs possess prey drive in varying degrees.* \*\*

**Submit:** To commit to the discretion or decisions of others.

\*\* *In order to maintain your alpha status, you must be able to make your dog submissive to you and your family.* \*\*

**Training:** The act, process, or method of one who trains; the knowledge or experience of one who trains.

\*\* *This process trains you, your dog, and your entire family on how to use the basic techniques and proper leash control.* \*\*

| Basic Obedience | Week 1 | Week 2 | Week 3 | Week 4 | Week 5 | Week 6 | Week 7 | Week 8 |
|---|---|---|---|---|---|---|---|---|
| OUT | | | | | | | | |
| COME | | | | | | | | |
| SIT | | | | | | | | |
| HEEL | | | | | | | | |
| DOWN | | | | | | | | |
| RETURN TO SIT | | | | | | | | |
| RETURN TO HEEL | | | | | | | | |
| SIT-WAIT | | | | | | | | |
| DOWN-WAIT | | | | | | | | |
| WAIT AT CURBS | | | | | | | | |
| WAIT AT DOORS | | | | | | | | |
| WALK-SIT | | | | | | | | |
| WALK-DOWN | | | | | | | | |
| COME & WAIT | | | | | | | | |
| LONG LEASH | | | | | | | | |
| TAB WORK | | | | | | | | |
| **BEHAVIOR MODIFICATION** | | | | | | | | |
| POISON PROOFING | | | | | | | | |
| MOUTHING | | | | | | | | |
| JUMPING | | | | | | | | |
| ESCAPING | | | | | | | | |
| CHEWING | | | | | | | | |
| HOUSEBREAKING | | | | | | | | |
| STEALING FOOD | | | | | | | | |
| NO & OK | | | | | | | | |
| | | | | | | | | |
| | | | | | | | | |

S=START          P=POOR          F=FAIR          G=GOOD          E=EXCELLENT

**CHECK YOUR PROGRESS**

# About the Author

     Frederick Woodard has had an established reputation as an animal behaviorist and master trainer in southeastern Michigan for the last 12 years. He began his career as a kennel trainer in the mid -1980's, teaching obedience and behavior modification at various dog training facilities in the state of Arizona under the tutelage of his mentor (a master trainer and former judge for the National Association of Protection Dogs). By 1988, Fred had begun working with the general public on curbing behavior problems and reaching obedience levels with their dogs.

The depth of Frederick's experience includes basic kennel training, group classes, individualized in-home training, and more. He has worked with a number of commercial enterprises in film work, has trained guard dogs, and is well-known among law enforcement groups for his highly-specialized skills and knowledge and his ability to achieve desired training goals. His other projects include working with canine aggressors of all breeds and taking training to a whole new level for personal protection.

Currently, Frederick owns and operates **K-9 Concepts**, a Michigan-based company formed in 1994, whose specialty is in-home dog training. Frederick and the K-9 Concepts staff work with students on an individual basis in their homes, explaining and demonstrating methods of proper interaction, behavior modification, and training techniques perfected through his twenty-plus years of experience. He and his staff are frequently recommended by veterinarians and other pet professionals to solve unwanted behavior problems from housebreaking to aggression. The company boasts a success rate of 98% and continues to grow.

**<u>Gotta Do Somethin' 'Bout that Dog!</u>** is a compilation of Frederick's many years of personal experience and an attempt to share his knowledge of canine behavior, which applies to dogs of all breeds, temperaments and backgrounds.

Printed in the United States
52998LVS00001B/90

9 781418 400118